CYNTHIA BENTZEN-MERCER

PhD, MBA, *USA Today* Bestselling Author

Human CAPITAL INVESTMENT STRATEGY

SIX STEPS TO

Cultivate Potential

AND YIELD COMPETITIVE ADVANTAGE

www.amplifypublishing.com

Human Capital Investment Strategy: Six Steps to
Cultivate Potential and Yield Competitive Advantage

For more information, please contact:
Amplify Publishing, an imprint of Amplify Publishing Group
620 Herndon Parkway, Suite 220
Herndon, VA 20170
info@amplifypublishing.com

LCCN: 2025917799

CPSIA: PRV1125A

ISBN: 979-8-89138-725-6

Printed in the United States

Dedication

In loving memory of my daddy, James (Jim) Michael Bentzen. Thank you for your loving support in life and in spirit. (1947 – 2024)

In honor of my mom, Linda K. Bax. I am deeply grateful for your endless encouragement to fulfill my most significant potential.

TABLE OF *Contents*

FOREWORD

Foreword

BY HEATHER E. MCGOWAN
KEYNOTE SPEAKER, *FORBES* TOP FUTURIST, BESTSELLING AUTHOR OF *THE ADAPTATION ADVANTAGE* AND *THE EMPATHY ADVANTAGE*

Cynthia and I first crossed paths when her organization brought me in to keynote for a team of healthcare executives. What struck me immediately wasn't just her impressive experience but the infectious optimism and unwavering enthusiasm she brought to every conversation. We discovered an instant alignment—shared values, mutual conviction that ideas can change the world, and a relentless drive to unleash human potential through our writing and speaking.

Through subsequent book launches and speaking engagements across the globe, we've remained in contact, challenging each other's thinking while championing each other's missions. When Cynthia asked me to write this foreword, I was simultaneously stunned by the honor and thrilled by the opportunity. She is my sister-in-arms in the fight to transform how organizations think about their people.

What you'll discover in these pages isn't just another business framework—it's a manifesto from one of the most innovative minds I know. Cynthia has done what few thought leaders achieve: She's created a bridge between visionary thinking and practical implementation. Her Human Capital Investment Strategy doesn't just challenge conventional wisdom; it demolishes it and rebuilds something far more powerful in its place.

Here's a preview of the revolutionary perspectives we share, beautifully articulated through Cynthia's groundbreaking contribution to our shared vision of a world where human potential is the ultimate competitive advantage.

Human CAPITAL STRATEGY:
From Cog to Conductor

For centuries, we've built our economic systems on a fundamental misconception: that humans are inefficient machines to be managed as liabilities alone. This outdated thinking, born in the Industrial Revolution when workers were interchangeable parts in a production machine, has persisted through the Information Age and into our current AI era—despite overwhelming evidence that human talent has become our primary driver of economic value.

Labor evolved from being augmented by animal and mechanical power in agricultural societies, to being subordinated to machinery in industrial eras, to becoming the dominant cost in knowledge work. Today, in our AI-augmented world, human capital represents the critical differentiator. As I have said for more than a decade, we need to stop viewing humans as a cost to contain and treat them as an asset to develop. By categorizing humans as a mere liability to be managed, we are constraining the very resource most essential to navigating persistent uncertainty: human ingenuity.

Cynthia Bentzen-Mercer argues in these pages that human capital is the most underleveraged asset in business. We've spent decades miscategorizing humans as liabilities. We needed a book—a guide, a set of frameworks—to think about human talent as a strategic driver to be developed as an appreciating asset. That guide is now in your hands.

THE *Efficiency* TRAP THAT BECAME OUR FRAGILITY

Our obsession with efficiency—what has become "hyper-efficiency"—has created dangerous vulnerability. We optimized every task, moment, and activity for predictability and profit, believing that efficiency equaled profitability. Ironically, we only measured what we knew how to measure: easily quantifiable components of busy work or hours spent, neither of which necessarily indicate value created or progress made.

The pandemic exposed this thinking as fundamentally flawed. When supply chains collapsed and fears led to shortages, we discovered that our pursuit of efficiency had eliminated the redundancy and adaptability we needed most. We valued predictability over adaptability, capability over potential, performance over purpose—building organizations optimized for yesterday's challenges while being woefully unprepared for tomorrow's opportunities.

Bentzen-Mercer's framework directly addresses this fragility. Her Talent Risk Index helps organizations quantify their exposure to risks like succession gaps, turnover sensitivity, and skills concentration—the very vulnerabilities that hyper-efficiency creates. By stratifying risk across retention likelihood, strategic criticality, and replacement difficulty, leaders can build the resilience that efficiency alone cannot provide.

FIVE ERAS, ONE *Truth:*
Technology Amplifies Human Potential

Throughout human history—from hunter-gatherer collaboration

through agricultural communities, industrial production, and information work—each era has revealed the same fundamental truth: Technology is only as good as the humans who use it. Will we reach Artificial General Intelligence (AGI) that finally supplants human ingenuity? Maybe, but unlikely. Humans will still play an increasingly important role doing what we do best: forming questions, making meaning, providing context, and making connections.

The agricultural era spanned over 7,000 generations. The industrial era lasted just six generations. The information era encompassed 1-2 generations. Now, for the first time in human history, a single generation will not only span multiple eras but work across them. This unprecedented acceleration means success no longer depends on stored knowledge or past expertise, but on the ability to learn, unlearn, and continuously adapt.

Artificial intelligence can store knowledge and engineer past experience, but it struggles to make meaning and understand context. Optimizing the human role in this realm of rising capabilities requires exactly what Bentzen-Mercer provides: strategic foresight, intentional investment, and the systematic crafting of diverse teams that can harness both synthetic and organic cognition to create sustainable economic value.

THE NEW *Success* PROFILE:
From Know-It-All to Learn-It-All

This reality demands a fundamental shift in how we think about talent—a shift that Bentzen-Mercer's framework directly supports. We're moving from hiring for past skills and experience to seeking individuals with behaviors that signal adaptability: curiosity, proactive tendencies, and the grit to wrestle through friction while knowing when to pivot. As a result, I predict a shift from a hyperfocus on closing the skills gap to embracing a pursuit of narrowing the skills gap while focusing on hiring for behaviors. A skills gap forms when a human demonstrates a skill and the market values that skill in excess of supply, creating a shortage or a gap. Viewed this way, a skills gap demonstrates progress if we remain in pursuit of narrowing it over time as it continues to push our capabilities to new frontiers. In this reality, behaviors of learning, unlearning, adaptation, and persistence are paramount.

Traditional hiring methods—gut instinct and résumé reviews—have embarrassingly low predictive validity ($r = 0.22$). Bentzen-Mercer advocates for structured interviews and validated assessments that measure non-teachable attributes like adaptability, leadership, and emotional intelligence, achieving much higher predictive validity ($r = 0.50$).

The most successful leaders are no longer unquestioned experts who make decisions with absolute certainty. Instead, they're humble, curious learners who use empathy to connect with multigenerational, pluralistic workforces and harness collective intelligence. Extensive research shows that companies with greater social, economic, cultural, and cognitive diversity excel at problem-solving and innovation, delivering superior economic returns.

This requires what Bentzen-Mercer calls diversification as a competitive advantage. Her data shows that companies in the top quartile for ethnic and cultural diversity are 36% more likely to outperform their peers in profitability. But achieving this requires leaders adept at processing diverse inputs, managing creative friction, and providing psychological safety—exactly the skills her Human Capital Performance Matrix helps identify and develop.

THE AUGMENTATION *Advantage:*

Humans and AI as Partners

We stand at a crossroads. Dystopian predictions about humans becoming "meat robots" serve only to spark fear and miss the extraordinary opportunity before us. In the augmented era, technology doesn't replace human capabilities—it amplifies them. The question isn't whether AI will make humans obsolete, but how we'll strategically combine human ingenuity with technological power.

This partnership requires us to rethink everything: what to automate versus augment, how to build on uniquely human advantages, and why the future belongs to organizations that place adaptability at their core. Success will come to those who transform their distinctly human capabilities—adaptability, empathy, and curiosity—into strategic advantages.

Bentzen-Mercer's framework provides the road map for this transformation. Her dynamic forecasting approach evolves workforce planning from static spreadsheets to real-time, intelligence-driven models that anticipate skill gaps, succession risks, and emerging talent needs. As she demonstrates with Target Canada's $5.4 billion loss from poor workforce planning, the cost of getting this wrong is catastrophic.

THE PATH *Forward:*

From Managing to Cultivating

The trillion-dollar question isn't whether humans are valuable—it's how we strategically invest in our primary driver of economic value. This requires a fundamental shift from managing humans as costs to cultivating human potential as capital.

Bentzen-Mercer's six-step Human Capital Investment Strategy provides the precise framework organizations need: establishing pro formas for human capital returns, assessing talent portfolios, stratifying risk, rebalancing allocations, expanding options through diversity, and forecasting dynamically. Her approach recognizes that employees are active investors of their human capital, choosing where to allocate their skills for the greatest personal return.

Her framework also addresses the motivational dimension through Daniel Pink's intrinsic motivators—autonomy, mastery, purpose, and recognition. While hygiene factors like competitive pay prevent dissatisfaction, they don't inspire greatness. True performance comes from treating motivation as the strategic asset it is.

We must rethink how we hire (for learning ability over past experience), how we develop (building adaptive capacity over fixed skills), how we reward (intrinsic motivation over compliance), and how we lead (empowerment over management). Most importantly, we must stop treating people as parts in a machine and start seeing them as the engine of transformation.

THE STRATEGIC IMPERATIVE OF *Human Potential*

The companies that thrive in the coming decades won't be those with the most sophisticated technology but those who unlock the full potential of the humans who wield that technology. Bentzen Mercer has provided the definitive guide for this transformation, reframing human capital as a strategic asset class that demands the same rigor as financial investments.

By embedding predictive analytics, diversification, and dynamic forecasting into workforce planning, organizations can unlock compounding returns in performance, innovation, and retention. Success hinges on the cultural transformation she advocates: making investing in people a core business strategy supported by continuous evaluation and reinvestment.

If you're ready to transform your greatest expense into your greatest competitive advantage, the road map is in your hands. The question isn't whether you can afford to implement these strategies—it's whether you can afford not to.

-Heather E. McGowan

Preface

*"Out beyond ideas of wrongdoing and rightdoing,
there is a field. I'll meet you there."*

—RUMI

Beyond the binaries—profit or purpose, performance or people—there is a space I have lived my life in: the space of both/and.

I was born into juxtaposition—southern California and rural Missouri, broadcast communications and an MBA, corporate and consulting, heart and mind. My career has never been about choosing sides. It has been about building bridges between disciplines, perspectives, and, most of all, people.

Over more than 30 years in executive leadership, I have observed a persistent gap: We manage money with strategy and structure but people with hope and habit. We revere assets on a spreadsheet but neglect the assets that walk through our doors every day.

There is a profound misalignment between how organizations manage financial capital and how they manage the human capital that individuals bring to work every day. That gap is costing companies real value.

I believe organizations do not just employ people—they are *entrusted* with their potential. When individual human capital is recognized, aligned, and strategically deployed, performance accelerates, cultures shift, and lives change. Every time we fail to invest in people, we leave value and impact on the table.

Human Capital Investment Strategy offers a finance-based, evidence-driven framework for managing people and their human capital as high-yield assets. This is not about performative leadership or feel-good culture. It is about operationalizing the collective human capital as a true source of competitive advantage.

While I am certain that every individual possesses unique human capital, I have not written this book solely from personal conviction. I have written it from the vantage point of three decades in global, cross-industry leadership—as a strategist, business executive, and social psychologist—having witnessed the massive untapped potential in every organization I have served.

....

HERE IS WHAT THAT *experience* HAS TAUGHT ME:

Human capital is the most underleveraged asset in business.

Every individual holds a portfolio of knowledge, skills, and natural strengths. The highest ROI comes not from fixing weaknesses, but from aligning and investing in strengths.

Peak performance is a function of alignment.

Human capital appreciates in value when people are placed in the right roles, and it deteriorates when misaligned. Today's workforce knows its agency. People are no longer passive resources; they are active investors, allocating their human capital where it earns the greatest return.

Diversification and meritocracy are not at odds.

Inherent talent is indiscriminate. When organizations apply

investment discipline to human capital, they mitigate bias and unlock greater potential.

Unlike financial assets, people can walk.
When undervalued, people will take their appreciating worth elsewhere. But when organizations invest wisely, treating people like the blue-chip assets they are, they not only retain them and their human capital but also unleash exponential growth.

THIS WORK IS NOT FOR THE FAINT OF HEART.

It is not an aspirational theory or leadership lip service. It is grounded in science, rooted in behavioral evidence, and forged through decades of real-world experience. It demands intellectual courage—the willingness to question legacy beliefs, to resist the comfort of either/or thinking, and to lead with both rigor and humanity. If you are ready to unlock the full potential of human capital—and realize the economic advantage that comes from embracing the power of both/and—then you are in the right place. Let's get to work.

INTRODUCTION

Introduction

*You can't expect capital-level returns if you
manage investments in people like maintenance costs.*

LET'S BEGIN WITH THE BOTTOM LINE

**Ifyou invest in your human capital with the same rigor
as your financial portfolio, you can expect:**

1. A force multiplier for performance
2. A more robust pool of human capital to source
3. Top decile employee and customer engagement
4. Greater protection from market volatility
5. Increased net operating income

Did that get your attention?

It should have—because the harsh reality is that most companies
are facing significant headwinds. Organizations are competing
for the same small talent pool. According to Gartner, employee
engagement is at an all-time low, the economic outlook is uncertain, and operating costs are cutting deeper into returns.

After 35 years of working as a human capital strategist with global
organizations, I have found that the professed belief in employees
as valuable assets is often, at best, conditional—though I do not necessarily believe it is an act of hypocrisy. Leaders want to believe it.

The issue is much more fundamental: The principle itself is flawed.

Employees are rewarded when earnings are strong, the economy is thriving, and business is booming. Fat and happy, companies generously compete for talent, rarely scrutinizing the return on their investment in the workforce. However, when the tide turns—earnings slip, costs rise, or markets falter—the "most valuable assets" become expendable. Companies proclaim that employees are their greatest asset; however, they are ultimately accounted for as a labor burden.

The financial premise behind *Human Capital Investment Strategy* is innovative, refocusing leadership on ushering in a new era of transformation. It moves beyond traditional organizational strategies toward a proactive, evidence-based approach that unlocks talent potential, builds cultures of excellence, enhances consumer experiences, and drives exceptional organizational performance.

It is time to stop merely *proclaiming* that employees are an organization's most valuable assets and start *actualizing* this with a bottom-line impact, **not because it is a nice thing to do but because it is the most fiscally responsible thing to do for all parties.**

A NEW *Approach*

Human Capital Investment Strategy is a practical, pragmatic, finance-based approach that strategically transforms human capital into a competitive advantage. It is not just about managing your workforce—it is about strategically investing in your people to drive business success. When applied purposefully, human capital investment becomes a force multiplier in building a high-performing, diversified workforce that serves as a powerful differentiator.

In the same way that sophisticated investors manage portfolios for long-term gain, today's business leaders must learn to manage human capital as an appreciating asset with asymmetric upside. This framework is built for executives who understand that financial returns are increasingly driven by talent strategy, not just capital structure.

This book is your playbook for doing just that.

PART ONE

IMPLEMENTING HUMAN CAPITAL INVESTMENT STRATEGY

We begin with the fundamentals of portfolio strategy, applied to human capital. These six steps help you transition from gut-driven decisions to disciplined human capital investment:

 1. Establish Pro Forma:

Articulate your investment thesis. Define the expected return on human capital in financial terms aligned with business strategy.

 2. Assess Portfolio:

Map your existing human capital allocation. Identify over-performers, underperformers, and hidden value across your workforce.

 3. Stratify Risk:

Quantify exposure to key-person risk, succession gaps, turn-over sensitivity, and skills concentration.

 4. Rebalance Allocations:

Adjust for underperforming segments and overexposed roles. Allocate resources where they generate alpha.

 5. Expand Options:

Integrate cognitive, experiential, and demographic diversification into your talent strategy to build resilience and adaptability.

 6. Forecast and Adjust:

Using workforce analytics, project future talent needs and reinvest in upskilling, mobility, and leadership pipelines with a forward-looking lens.

Each step turns strategy into execution. Beginning with data and evidence to support each step of the framework, leaders are provided with a comprehensive understanding of what is required and why it matters. Following each step, a detailed implementation outline is included. With checklists, decision tools, and investment criteria, leaders are equipped to act. No matter your company's stage or scale, this framework gives you the tools to make smarter talent bets, de-risk your leadership pipeline, and generate compounding returns over time.

PART TWO

ENABLING AN INVESTMENT CULTURE

Markets reward discipline—and so do talent systems. However, the real work of Human Capital Investment Strategy lies not in spreadsheets or frameworks, but in the organizational will to adopt a new mindset. An Organizational Readiness Assessment is included at the end of this section for those interested in understanding an organization's current readiness for transformation. This evaluation is also available online at **www.cynthiabentzenmercer.com/resources.**

This section focuses on creating a culture of investment across leadership. It demands executive resolve to move beyond legacy HR thinking and commit to a capital allocator's approach to people. It is required reading for any CEO who is serious about translating vision into enterprise value.

You cannot delegate this shift. It is a boardroom-level initiative that must be owned and championed by the entire executive team. Like any capital strategy, human capital investment requires top-down alignment, a tolerance for short-term discomfort, and an appetite for long-term gain.

TIME IS *Money*

Since the primary reader is a CEO or senior executive with limited time and high expectations, this book is designed to be clear, prescriptive, and immediately actionable. However, make no mistake: Brevity does not equal ease. The Human Capital Investment Strategy is a rigorous framework that demands strategic execution, executive commitment, and organizational alignment.

Human Capital Investment Strategy challenges you to lead like an investor—to think in terms of returns, operate intentionally, and recognize that your highest-yielding asset is not found on a balance sheet. It is sitting across the table, embedded in your teams, and leading your customer experience.

This approach requires conviction, resilience, and a long-game mindset. Great investors do not panic during down days, and great leaders do not abandon strategy when the people side gets complex.

TIME IS MONEY.
LET'S PUT IT TO WORK.

PART ONE

PART ONE

IMPLEMENTING *Human* CAPITAL INVESTMENT STRATEGY

Prospectus

··

BACKGROUND

From Adam Smith's early observations on the wealth of nations to Peter Drucker's insights on knowledge workers, the concept that people possess human capital worthy of investment has evolved in tandem with economic and technological advancements. Today, human capital is no longer measured merely in terms of education or skills but in the ability of individuals to learn, adapt, and thrive within an organization's unique ecosystem. Businesses have recognized the power of **human capital portfolio, their workforce's collective will, abilities, knowledge, skills, and talents,** as the driving force behind economic and organizational success.

In economic terms, human capital is much more than a theoretical concept—it is a measurable financial asset. Businesses rely on financial capital to fund operations and growth, but human capital determines how effectively that financial capital is deployed. Studies consistently show that companies with highly engaged and well-developed workforces outperform their competitors in profitability, innovation, and long-term stability.

Organizations with a strategic approach to human capital investment see tangible financial returns. **Research by the McKinsey Global Institute has shown that companies with strong human capital strategies generate shareholder returns that are 2.5**

times higher than their industry peers. Gallup has found that businesses with engaged employees experience 21% higher profitability, 17% higher productivity, and 40% lower turnover than those who fail to invest in their workforce.

However, despite overwhelming evidence that human capital drives financial performance, many organizations treat it as solely an operational expense rather than an appreciating asset. This outdated mindset is a relic of the industrial era, when workers were seen as interchangeable labor rather than the intellectual and creative force behind an organization's success. However, labor is no longer a commodity in a world where innovation cycles are short, talent markets are global, and the shelf life of skills is shrinking.

HUMAN CAPITAL IS THE
COMPETITIVE ADVANTAGE
—if you know how to invest in it.

PROBLEM

The problem:
We attempt to apply an *altruistic* principle to a *financial* equation, relying on our gut instead of statistics.

The misalignment between financial and human capital strategies is not a simple oversight; it is a structural failure in how organizations allocate resources to their most valuable asset. It is not about culture for culture's sake; it is about a fundamental investment blind spot on the organizational balance sheet, where individual human capital remains undervalued, underleveraged, and strategically ignored.

Consider for a moment that every person possesses a unique combination of will, abilities, knowledge, skills, talents—their human capital. Just like any other asset, human capital has inherent value. To the extent that a person's human capital is well-aligned with the role and the organization, exceptional performance drives increased value.

The prevailing approach to workforce management treats employees as an expense to be controlled rather than an asset to be cultivated. As a result, businesses inadvertently undermine their long-term success by failing to apply the same strategic discipline to human capital as other forms of capital.

To illustrate, business leaders have meticulously scrutinized financial investments, real estate acquisitions, product development, and operational efficiencies for decades, ensuring that every dollar is allocated to maximize returns. However, when investing in their workforce—the engine that drives innovation, customer satisfaction, and long-term profitability—many organizations fall back on outdated assumptions, reactive decision-making, or simply delegating workforce strategy to the human resources department.

When financial capital and human capital strategies are disconnected, organizations face a range of predictable consequences: crisis hiring to address urgent talent shortages, reactionary layoffs in economic downturns, disengaged employees who see little incentive to contribute beyond baseline expectations, and a revolving door of talent attrition that erodes institutional knowledge. These are not mere symptoms of a volatile market; they are the direct result of a leadership mindset that bifurcates workforce investment from overall business strategy. However, it is more complex.

THERE ARE TWO CRITICAL *Differentiators* BETWEEN FINANCIAL CAPITAL AND HUMAN CAPITAL.

1. **Predictive modeling to assess future performance is strongly relied upon** in financial investing and grossly underutilized in human capital investing.

2. **Unlike financial assets, individuals have agency over their capital**—they choose where to invest their assets for the most significant personal return.

Shifting labor market dynamics and increasing expectations for meaningful work, competitive compensation, career development opportunities, and flexible work arrangements exacerbate the problem. The post-pandemic workforce no longer views a paycheck as sufficient motivation; they seek purpose, autonomy, and an organization that invests in their growth. In short, the rules of workforce engagement have evolved, but many organizations continue to operate under an outdated playbook.

PURPOSE

The organizations that thrive in today's economy recognize that a Human Capital Portfolio functions like financial assets, requiring strategic allocation, risk management, and long-term planning to maximize returns. Just as investors seek to diversify funds, hedge risks, and optimize growth, leaders must take a deliberate approach to talent acquisition, development, and retention.

A well-managed Human Capital Portfolio ensures that employees are qualified for their roles and positioned for maximum impact. Human capital investments compound over time, just like financial investments. Employees who receive continuous learning opportunities, meaningful career growth, and a sense of purpose contribute exponentially more to an organization's bottom line than those trained for a job and left to stagnate. **Companies that recognize this dynamic treat human capital not as a sunk cost, but as an appreciating asset that fuels long-term success.**

SOLUTION

The solution?:
Counterintuitive but clear: Invest in human capital with the same discipline, rigor, and predictive modeling as financial capital, and your organization will cultivate *potential* and yield a *sustainable* competitive advantage.

Organizations require individuals' human capital to operate, innovate, and generate profit. Their success depends on attracting, developing, and retaining the right Human Capital Portfolio and investing in these assets.

Companies that align the right human capital in the right roles and create an environment where they can flourish benefit from a portfolio that outperforms the market. It is a fundamental economic proposition. People bring human capital that businesses need to survive. Leaders must learn to utilize data and science to develop a peak-performing portfolio of human capital and create an environment where every valuable asset chooses to put their gifts to work.

Human CAPITAL INVESTMENT STRATEGY
REFRAMES WORKFORCE PLANNING THROUGH THE LENS OF CAPITAL INVESTMENT.

It enables CEOs and senior leaders to treat human capital as a high-yield, appreciating asset class that requires the same rigor, discipline, and performance management as any financial portfolio. The strategy comprises six integrated steps designed to align human capital decisions with organizational growth, agility, and strategic returns.

STEP 1
Establish Pro Forma

- Define human capital as a strategic asset.
- Link workforce planning to macroeconomic and organizational strategy.
- Identify capabilities required to meet short- and long-term goals.
- Build a formal pro forma template to guide human capital investments.

STEP 2
Assess Portfolio

- Assess performance, potential, and workforce composition.
- Use data-driven, bias-mitigated assessments.
- Visualize human capital on performance/potential quadrants.
- Operationalize evaluation as a recurring executive process.

STEP 3
Stratify Risk

- Identify exposure across five risk types: talent, potential, flight, depth, and diversity.
- Use a structured risk-scoring model.
- Translate findings into mitigation plans aligned with business continuity.

STEP 4
Rebalance Allocations

- Redirect resources based on portfolio insights.
- Exit or reposition underperformers.
- Accelerate high-growth human capital and optimize top talent.
- Normalize rebalancing as a strategic discipline.

STEP 5
Expand Options

- Redefine selection criteria to focus on predictive potential.
- Leverage structured hiring and validated assessments.
- Proactively source from nontraditional and diverse pipelines.
- Enhance early integration through onboarding and mentorship.

STEP 6
Forecast & Adjust

- Build a real-time forecasting engine tied to strategic planning.
- Track key metrics and model future needs.
- Institutionalize agility through governance and adjustment protocols.

Each step is not a standalone initiative but part of an integrated, iterative process of continuous assessment, refinement, and reinvestment cycle of the individuals and the human capital portfolio. Just as financial markets fluctuate and talent dynamics shift, organizations that fail to adjust will find themselves at a competitive disadvantage.

Part Two has been included to support enabling a Human Capital Investment Strategy culture, recognizing the significant change required to move from legacy thinking to an investment mindset.

SIGNIFICANCE

The time to move to a Human Capital Investment Strategy is *now*.

Rapid technological advancements, shifting demographic trends, and an increasingly complex global economy define the modern business environment. Companies that fail to recognize the importance of human capital as a strategic investment will find themselves at a competitive disadvantage, unable to attract and retain the talent necessary for innovation and growth.

This book is about shifting mindsets from relying on hunches to demanding predictive analytics. It is about applying investment principles—diversification, compounding value, and risk management—to grow, lead, and leverage talent. When organizations treat individuals' human capital like a valuable portfolio—an asset class with measurable return—they gain clarity and a lasting competitive advantage.

STEP ONE

ESTABLISH PRO FORMA

**Human capital isn't a sunk cost—
it's an appreciating asset.**

At 5:34 p.m. on May 22, 2011, the city of Joplin, Missouri, was hit by a catastrophic EF-5 tornado. With a path extending 22 miles, a width of nearly a mile at its widest point, and wind speeds surpassing 200 mph, the tornado tore through the heart of Joplin, devastating a significant portion of the city, including the downtown business district, residential areas, and critical infrastructure.

As the tornado tore through the heart of Joplin, devastating a large portion of the city, Mercy's 367-bed hospital took a direct hit. At the time, approximately 183 patients and more than 400 staff members were inside. Caregivers heroically shielded immobile patients with their own bodies, navigated darkened and debris-filled stairwells to evacuate the injured, and quickly established makeshift triage areas in parking lots and nearby buildings. Despite the hospital's catastrophic structural damage, including the loss of its power supply, water, and medical records, staff evacuated every patient. Sadly, yet miraculously, only four ventilator-dependent patients lost their lives.

While clinicians are trained for crisis, the magnitude of this tragedy spanned well beyond the events of May 22. A total of 158 people perished, over 1,150 were injured, and more than 9,000 residents were displaced. In a town of approximately 50,000 people, nearly everyone was affected somehow, whether through the loss of loved ones, homes, businesses, or a sense of security.

As the third-largest employer in the city of Joplin, in the aftermath, a pressing concern was the fate of the hospital's employees. Within 24 hours of the devastating event, Mercy's CEO, Lynn Britton, made a bold commitment: No one would lose their job as long as they were willing and able to remain in Joplin and lend their skills and talents where needed. The hospital would be rebuilt, and in the meantime, every employee, from nurses to maintenance staff, would continue receiving paychecks, even as operations were relocated to smaller temporary facilities.

For the 2,200 employees, the traditional work structure, where roles were clearly defined and responsibilities neatly assigned, disappeared almost instantly. However, housekeepers, environmental services teams, food service employees, administrators, nurses, doctors, and other hospital staff—many of whom had lost their homes—set aside their titles and tapped into something more profound: their human capital. They assessed what was needed and adapted, leveraging their skills, knowledge, and service commitment. People stepped up without a physical hospital to report to, formal systems to operate within, or clear directives.

A surgeon who had spent years in an operating room now found herself treating the injured at a makeshift triage center. A nurse, previously confined to a specific department, transitioned into a hotline crisis coordinator, directing patients and volunteers. Once tied to desks and spreadsheets, administrative staff became logistical masterminds, securing supplies and organizing efforts to restore critical services. Maintenance and environmental services staff coordinated donations of bottled water, blankets, and equipment. Strangers became teammates in a spontaneous workforce that rebuilt a hospital and a lifeline.

The devastation in Joplin revealed an unexpected truth: Even when buildings crumble and systems fail, human capital is the true engine of recovery. The knowledge, skills, adaptability, and intrinsic motivation of people—these intangible assets—became the bedrock for rebuilding. Without physical infrastructure or defined roles, individuals stepped forward, not because of a paycheck but because of purpose. Joplin's swift economic recovery became a national example of resilience, powered by leadership, coordinated action, and a deep investment in people.

· ·

HUMAN *Assets*

At the time of the tornado, I had been with Mercy for just five months, serving as the head of human resources for the health system. What unfolded in the following weeks and months profoundly shaped my understanding of workforce value. The investment in each person—the space to lead, adapt, and apply their strengths—fueled the rebuilding of a hospital, a community, and a regional economy.

This experience underscored a vital principle: Human capital is not just a resource but the primary driver of organizational resilience and performance. However, while organizations routinely invest in physical assets like technology, real estate, and equipment, they rarely approach human capital with the same strategic discipline.

Like financial planning, human capital investment requires intentionality—deciding where to allocate resources, manage risk, and optimize return. Without a structured investment strategy, leaders often default to what feels safe or familiar, overlooking growth opportunities, misallocating talent, and falling short of their potential.

THIS IS WHERE THE HUMAN CAPITAL INVESTMENT STRATEGY (HCIS) COMES INTO PLAY.

Just as financial planning starts with data—understanding market conditions, assessing risks, and setting long-term objectives—HCIS requires the same level of rigor. Without data-driven insights and strategic foresight, organizations risk making reactive, short-term decisions that do not fully leverage their workforce's potential.

Success in human capital investment starts with reliable information, clear performance indicators, and a well-defined strategic direction. This foundational step enables informed decision-making and ensures that human capital investments produce meaningful returns, just as they do in other areas of business.

··

HUMAN CAPITAL INVESTMENT STRATEGY *Pro Forma*

Step One begins with establishing an HHCISro Forma, beginning with understanding the macroeconomic and microeconomic factors and the organization's short-term and long-term objectives.

A common mistake leaders make is jumping directly to people metrics, overlooking the link between human capital performance and business results. Unless your business operates uniquely without human labor, ultimately, the people will be responsible for achieving organizational outcomes.

The top half of the pro forma focuses on economic and organizational performance data. This includes revenue growth targets, margin expansion goals, market share expectations, innovation pipelines, and other financial or strategic benchmarks that define enterprise value. These indicators serve as the "why" behind human capital investments—the strategic context against which all people-related decisions should be evaluated. Care must be taken to ensure that forecasts and predictions rely on trustworthy sources and thorough insights. Industry associations often have their finger on the pulse of government relations and advocacy, providing valuable perspective.

The bottom half of the pro forma translates those organizational goals into human capital performance indicators—the "how." This is where talent strategy becomes capital strategy. By combining business insights and trends with desired performance outcomes, we can create a comprehensive and well-informed HCIS Pro Forma.

....

Macro AND *Micro* TRENDS

In almost every boardroom and meeting room around the globe, leaders regularly assess their organizations' financial health by using metrics such as return on equity (ROE), return on investment (ROI), net operating income (NOI), EBITDA, revenue growth, earnings growth, and market position. Furthermore, most leaders are knowledgeable about monitoring the macro-economic landscape, including gross domestic product (GDP), inflation rates, interest rates, the consumer confidence index, government policies, geopolitical events, stock and bond trends, market volatility, and industry-specific changes.

With this information, multimillion-dollar decisions are made. However, despite relying on human capital to achieve performance outcomes, most companies fail to integrate workforce analytics into their strategic planning. Instead of evaluating employment trends, workforce capabilities, and organizational readiness alongside financial metrics, leadership often relegates all people-related matters to the human resources department. This separation is a critical mistake.

By separating human capital strategy from financial capital strategy, companies prepare themselves for reactionary decision-making, crisis hiring to address sudden consumer demand, or impulsive layoffs to counter disappointing returns. Without a clear understanding of how the workforce is aligned to support business goals, strategic plans are, at best, incomplete and, at worst, destined to fail.

Recognizing human capital as a strategic asset demands a disciplined approach that integrates key workforce indicators into ongoing performance reviews with the same rigor as financial reporting. As labor market conditions change, workforce analysis and reporting must occur as frequently as all other capital assessments.

The following pages outline key macroeconomic trends. Depending on when this book is read, the economic factors discussed will serve as both a prospectus for current opportunities and a historical reference for workforce trends, assisting leaders in making informed, forward-thinking investments in human capital. **This data outlines why HCIS is not a nice idea but a critical business imperative.**

MACROECONOMIC
F A C T O R S

e.g., Change in consumer habits

MICROECONOMIC
F A C T O R S

e.g., Shrinking margins

Labor TRENDS

In recent decades, the U.S. population growth has outpaced that of the labor force, primarily due to an aging demographic. This demographic shift is expected to persist over the next decade, further widening the gap between population and labor force growth.

Specifically, the labor force is projected to grow at an annual rate of 0.5%, which is slower than the 0.8% annual growth forecast for the overall population (U.S. Bureau of Labor Statistics). Consequently, the labor force participation rate, which measures the proportion of the working-age population that is either employed or actively seeking work, is expected to decline steadily from 61.7% in 2020 to 60.4% by 2030. This represents a loss of approximately $3.4 million in workforce participation.

This ongoing divergence between population growth and labor force expansion reflects broader demographic shifts, such as the retirement of the baby boomer generation and a slowdown in immigration rates. These trends pose significant challenges for workforce planning, economic growth, and talent acquisition strategies, as organizations may face a smaller pool of available workers.

As the population ages and fewer individuals join the labor force, businesses must adapt by exploring new avenues for workforce engagement, automation, and talent development to maintain productivity and competitiveness.

While some of the gap will be addressed through AI and other emerging technologies, automation is not a wholesale substitute for human capital. AI will undoubtedly reshape tasks, augment decision-making, and increase efficiency in certain roles, but it will also create new demand for skills in oversight, judgment, innovation, and human connection. Rather than eliminating the need for people, AI is redefining what people are needed for. This shift amplifies the importance of strategic workforce planning, upskilling, and role redesign. **Organizations that treat AI as a copilot rather than a replacement will be better positioned to navigate the demographic shortfall, protect institutional knowledge, and unlock new forms of value from their existing talent portfolios.** In this way, technology becomes a lever for resilience, not a crutch for shrinking labor.

GENDER

According to the U.S. Census Bureau, women's labor force participation increased significantly during the latter half of the 20th century, representing a notable shift in the labor market. From the 1960s to the 1980s, participation rose sharply before slowing in the 1990s, peaking at 60.0% in 1999. A gradual decline followed, accelerated after the 2007–2009 recession, and stabilized around 2014. In 2020, labor force participation for women and men dropped sharply due to the COVID-19 pandemic but began to recover in 2022. Meanwhile, men's labor force participation has steadily declined since its 1948 peak of 86.6%.

Civilian Labor Force Participation by Sex, Annual Averages 1948 to Present

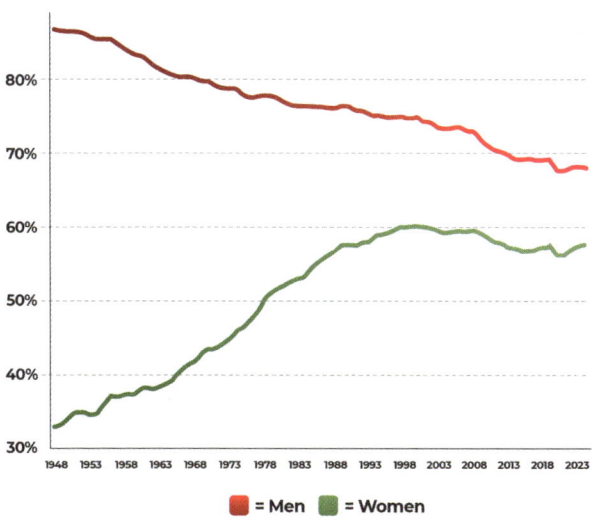

= Men   = Women

EDUCATION

During the 2021–2022 academic year, women made up 58% of total college enrollment in the United States, continuing a trend that has been widening since the 1980s. They earned 58.5% of all bachelor's degrees, 62.6% of master's degrees, and the majority of professional and doctoral degrees. These figures are consistent year over year and are accelerating across nearly every academic discipline and demographic category.

Notably, women now outpace men nearly two to one in earning advanced degrees across all racial and ethnic groups, including Black, Hispanic, Asian, and White student populations. This consistent advantage in higher education signals a significant long-term shift in the future leadership and professional pipeline.

Yet despite these gains, in 2024, women represented 47% of the workforce; however, they held only 29% of the top C-suite positions and 11% of the Fortune 500 CEO roles. This gap between credentials and corporate influence presents both a challenge and an opportunity for organizations ready to unlock the full value of their human capital.

Representation in Corporate Role by Gender and Race, % of Employees

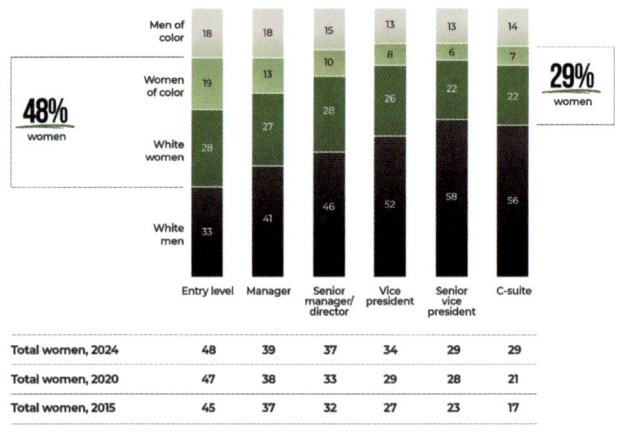

	Entry level	Manager	Senior manager/ director	Vice president	Senior vice president	C-suite
Total women, 2024	48	39	37	34	29	29
Total women, 2020	47	38	33	29	28	21
Total women, 2015	45	37	32	27	23	17

Source: McKinsey & Company and LeanIn.Org, 2024

Note:
Women surpass men in obtaining advanced degrees and make up nearly half of the available workforce, constituting an untapped human capital resource.

AGE

For several decades, workforce economists have predicted a significant talent shortage as baby boomers, born between 1946 and 1964, reach 65. This prediction began to materialize as the labor market shrank before COVID-19. After the pandemic, the combination of longer life expectancy and retirement planning shortfalls has led many individuals nearing retirement to reenter the workforce, temporarily delaying the inevitable. Ultimately, there is no avoiding the significant gap emerging when the last baby boomers turn 65 in 2030.

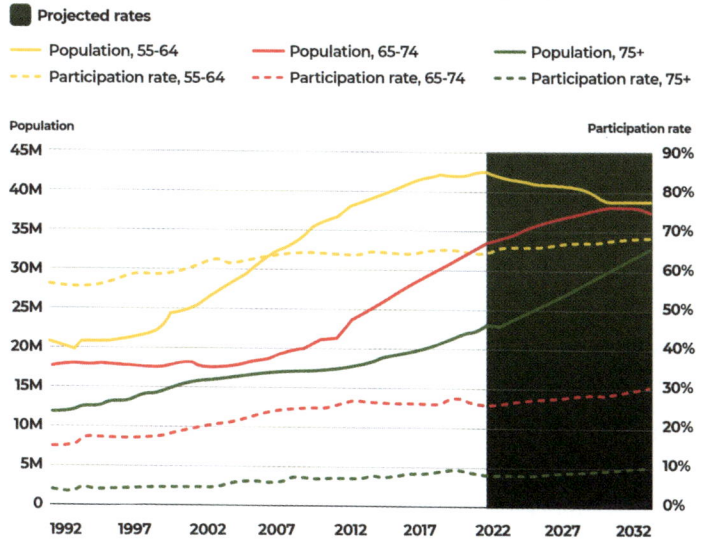

America's Workforce Is Aging

■ Projected rates

— Population, 55-64   — Population, 65-74   — Population, 75+
--- Participation rate, 55-64   --- Participation rate, 65-74   --- Participation rate, 75+

Source: U.S. Bureau of Labor Statistics, age groups 55+, 2023

The disruption is exacerbated by the slowdown in population growth in the United States. The U.S. witnessed a 10% growth from 2000 to 2010, which declined to 7.5% from 2010 to 2020. The projected population growth from 2020 to 2030 is 5.5%.

Note:
The U.S. Bureau of Labor Statistics projects that 6.7 million new jobs will be created by 2033. As demand rises and human capital becomes increasingly scarce, leveraging the full potential of all five generations in the workforce will be essential for business continuity and growth.

RACE/ETHNICITY

The demographic composition of the U.S. adult workforce has undergone notable shifts over the past few decades. In 2024, Hispanic workers represented 19% of the adult workforce, a significant increase from 12% in 2000. Asian workers made up 7%, rising from 4% in 2000. Conversely, the proportion of White workers fell to 60%, down from 71% in 2000. The percentage of Black workers remained relatively stable, with a slight rise to 12% in 2024 from 11% in 2000.

Looking ahead, the U.S. Bureau of Labor Statistics projects that this trend will continue through 2033. The labor force is expected to grow from approximately 167 million in 2023 to 173 million by 2033, representing a 3.6% increase. However, this growth will not occur uniformly across all demographic groups (U.S. Bureau of Labor Statistics).

- **Hispanic Workers:** The Hispanic labor force is projected to grow by 23.8% from 2023 to 2033, increasing from 28.6 million to 35.4 million. This growth rate is higher than any other major racial or ethnic group, reflecting ongoing demographic trends and immigration patterns.

- **Asian Workers:** The Asian labor force is projected to grow by 18.9% during the same period, increasing from 11.7 million to 13.9 million. This growth highlights the substantial contribution of Asian workers, specifically to sectors such as technology, healthcare, and engineering.

- **Black Workers:** The Black labor force is projected to grow modestly by 5.8%, increasing from 20.1 million to 21.3 million. While this indicates a rise, it remains relatively minor compared to other groups, highlighting ongoing challenges in workforce participation and employment equity.

- **White Workers:** The number of White workers is

projected to decrease by 2.3%, from 100.3 million to 98.1 million. This decline aligns with broader demographic trends, such as aging populations and lower birth rates among White communities.

> **Note:**
> **Labor force projections point to a steadily diversifying U.S. workforce, with Hispanic and Asian workers representing two of the fastest-growing segments. Rather than a demographic footnote, this shift is a strategic signal: Organizations that intentionally expand and tailor their recruitment efforts to reflect this diversity will be better positioned to thrive.**

Future OF WORK

Alongside the changing demographics of the workforce, the global economy has undergone a significant transformation over the past 25 years. Traditional industrial models have transitioned into a knowledge-based economy, where information, innovation, and human expertise are crucial. This shift has redefined workforce dynamics, organizational structures, and the skills necessary for success.

The ongoing shift to a knowledge economy is one of the most significant yet underestimated disruptions in the workforce. The rapid adoption of artificial intelligence and machine learning has already transformed how work is performed. As automation advances, jobs that depend on physical labor are becoming obsolete. Intellectual capabilities are rapidly emerging as the primary path to employment, growth, and wealth creation.

A knowledge economy portends a declining value of physical assets, emphasizing intellectual property. With fewer connections to bricks and mortar, this shift promotes the globalization of thoughts, ideas, innovations, and collaborations. For specific industries, the move to a knowledge economy has represented a seismic disruption; for others, it has been a more gradual evolution.

Companies are investing significant time and resources in automating processes, leveraging AI, and reducing their dependency on human labor to achieve cost-cutting and increased efficiency. While these efforts are commendable, insufficient attention is given to the HCIS, which must support a constantly evolving, decentralized, diverse, and highly specialized team of humans and machines.

As AI and automation take over more routine and rules-based tasks, the competitive edge moves squarely into human territory: ideation, emotional intelligence, adaptability, and leadership. In this context, the stakes for getting human capital decisions right have never been higher. Hiring for technical competence alone misses the point. The natural talent behind those technical layers drives long-term value, even more so in a technological world.

This is where goal setting comes into sharp focus. Leaders must stop asking "What roles do I need to fill?" and start asking "What irreplaceable human traits does my organization need to compete?" Without this shift, organizations risk building teams that look qualified on paper but lack the internal horsepower to adapt, innovate, and lead.

> **Note:**
> **The availability of skilled talent is becoming an increasingly defining factor in business success.** *Given the shrinking labor force, attracting and sourcing the right human capital attributes will be essential.*

Goal SETTING

In an ever-shifting economic environment, strategic goal setting isn't just a leadership exercise; it's the foundation for intentional human capital investment. Within the HCIS Pro Forma, both short- and long-term goals must be clearly articulated to shape workforce priorities, determine pacing, and define success.

SHORT-TERM GOALS

Short-term goals are typically aligned with the company's current market conditions, financial position, and operational agility.

These objectives might include:

- Increasing market share by 10%
- Launching a new product line within 12 months
- Entering a new customer segment or geographic region
- Reducing time-to-productivity for new hires
- Responding to a competitive disruption or regulatory change

Short-term targets help determine immediate human capital needs, such as hiring timelines, skill gaps, or interim leadership assignments. For example, if consumer preferences shift rapidly, the company may need to upskill frontline employees, restructure marketing talent, or diversify hiring pipelines to maintain relevance.

Rapid growth may create opportunities to leverage economies of scale, but only if the right talent infrastructure is in place. In this context, workforce planning becomes a real-time investment exercise: How quickly can the organization align capabilities to its operational goals?

LONG-TERM GOALS

Long-term goals set the strategic horizon for human capital deployment. These aspirations guide Steps Two through Six of the HCIS model, shaping decisions on talent acquisition, leadership development, succession planning, and retention investment.

Examples of long-term goals include:

- Doubling in size over three years
- Preparing for an IPO or merger
- Expanding into international markets
- Transforming the business model through digital innovation
- Creating a sustainable, multigenerational company culture

These ambitions demand a scalable and future-ready Human Capital Portfolio (HCP). For instance, a company planning for an IPO must ensure financial rigor and cultivate investor-ready leadership and governance. A firm pursuing longevity and legacy must build institutional knowledge, career pathways, and a resilient culture across all talent tiers.

STRATEGIC FIT WITH HCIS

At the outset of an HCIS journey, it is vital to codify short- and long-term objectives. Why? The human capital allocation strategy should mirror the capital allocation strategy, with clarity on where, when, and why to invest. Whether the aim is to stabilize in a volatile market or accelerate toward exponential growth, the goals define the HCP's risk tolerance, time horizon, and return expectations.

In addition to the company's size, complexity, and readiness, long-term organizational goals influence the pace at which you approach Steps Two through Six.

HUMAN CAPITAL PERFORMANCE *Indicators*

The HCIS Pro Forma is the executive's bridge between organizational ambition and workforce reality. Like any sound investment thesis, it begins with a clear understanding of success.

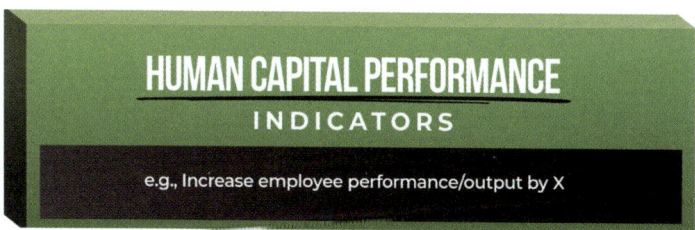

Key questions to consider in this section of the HCIS Pro Forma include:

- What outcomes must the HCP deliver to enable business strategy?

- Which roles, skills, and capabilities are most critical to achieving those outcomes?

- What is the workforce's current performance and future potential in those areas?

- Where are we overinvested or underexposed?

- What indicators will be used to track return on human capital investment over time?

- What systemic or structural impediments exist within the organization that will limit success if not addressed?

Just as financial investors track EBITDA, cash flow, and market multiples, human capital investors must track leading and lagging performance indicators. This is the only way to establish accountability, validate investment decisions, and continuously refine the portfolio for higher yield.

Ultimately, your human capital performance indicators define how people perform and how effectively your organization converts human capital into enterprise value.

SWOT ANALYSIS

A well-executed SWOT analysis is a critical early step in understanding the HCP requirements necessary to achieve organizational goals. Just as a financial portfolio requires an assessment of asset strength, volatility, and market forces, your human capital must be evaluated with the same discipline, evidence, and foresight.

This process uncovers the internal strengths and weaknesses within your talent systems and the external opportunities and threats that may accelerate or hinder strategic execution. It is not a cursory exercise—this diagnostic must be approached with humility, data, and candor.

Internal Strengths:
What existing assets give your workforce a competitive edge?

- A strong employment brand with high offer acceptance rates
- Robust leadership pipeline and succession depth
- Strong employee engagement and retention metrics
- High-performing, value-aligned teams
- Established learning and development infrastructure

Internal Weaknesses:
What internal gaps or inefficiencies limit workforce performance?

- Wage compression or uncompetitive compensation structures
- Skill shortages in critical functions
- Weak talent mobility or underinvestment in internal development
- Low trust in leadership or change fatigue
- Inconsistent people management capability

Evaluating internal factors should rely on quantifiable evidence, not assumptions. Leverage data from exit interviews, engagement surveys, performance distributions, internal promotion rates, and platforms like Glassdoor to assess how your organization is perceived and experienced by talent.

External Opportunities:
What macro or market conditions can be leveraged to build talent advantage?

- Increased number of recent graduates in relevant fields
- Remote work enabling access to broader talent pools
- Strategic partnerships with academic or training institutions
- Availability of funding for upskilling or apprenticeship programs
- Social and cultural momentum around purpose-driven work

External Threats:
What external risks could compromise your ability to attract, retain, or deploy talent?

- Tight labor markets and aging workforce demographics
- Increased poaching of critical roles by competitors
- Rising healthcare or benefits costs
- Technological disruption outpacing current capabilities
- Regulatory changes impacting labor classifications or compliance

STRATEGIC ROLE IN HCIS

The insights from your SWOT analysis serve as the diagnostic engine of the pro forma, helping you determine where to double down, where to de-risk, and where reallocation of human capital is required. It is as central to human capital strategy as a balance sheet is to financial strategy.

Moreover, this analysis sets the tone for Steps Two through Six of the HCIS framework by identifying:

- Which workforce segments require greater investment
- What structural risks need to be mitigated
- Where untapped value can be unlocked through pro-active planning

Organizations that treat SWOT as a checkbox miss its strategic power. Those who treat it as an investment-grade assessment of their workforce will make smarter, faster, and more informed decisions.

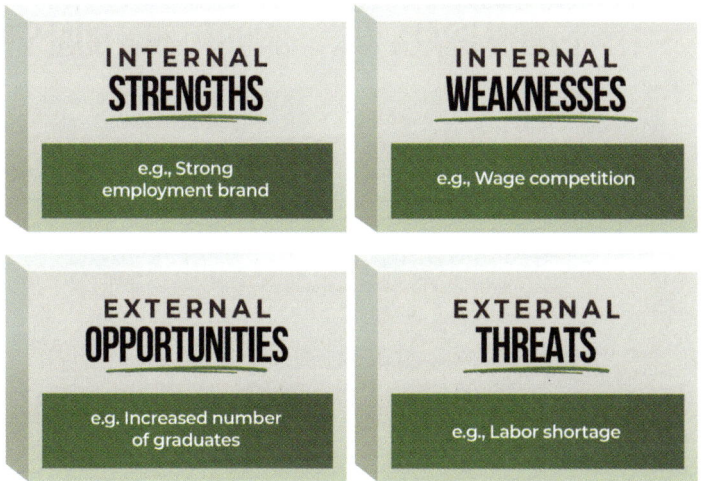

Recognizing external opportunities and threats to human capital is vital. Many business leaders fail to seize opportunities and waste time and resources managing threats. Opportunities encourage leaders to invest more significantly as we progress through the HCIS steps, while threats indicate where to pivot. Creating the pro forma is as crucial to HCIS as it is to financial planning.

HCIS PRO FORMA

MACROECONOMIC FACTORS
e.g., Change in consumer habits

MICROECONOMIC FACTORS
e.g., Shrinking margins

ORGANIZATIONS' LONG-TERM GOALS
e.g., Double in size within 3 years

ORGANIZATIONS' SHORT-TERM GOALS
e.g., Increase market share by 10%

HUMAN CAPITAL PERFORMANCE INDICATORS
e.g., Increase employee performance/output by X

INTERNAL STRENGTHS
e.g., Strong employment brand

INTERNAL WEAKNESSES
e.g., Wage competition

EXTERNAL OPPORTUNITIES
e.g. Increased number of graduates

EXTERNAL THREATS
e.g., Labor shortage

Conclusion

As we look ahead to an increasingly complex and uncertain future, the lessons from the Joplin tornado underscore a powerful truth: Strategic investment in human capital is not optional; it's foundational. When processes, systems, technology, and physical structure are removed, it is the people with human capital that carry forth the organization's mission.

Just as financial investments secure long-term success, organizations must invest intentionally in their people, recognizing that their abilities, knowledge, skills, and talents are valuable assets and catalysts for growth, resilience, and transformation.

Today's business environment—defined by a shrinking labor pool, demographic shifts, and the rise of a knowledge-based economy—presents both risks and opportunities. Organizations that proactively align human capital goals with macroeconomic and organizational objectives will be far better positioned to lead, innovate, and adapt.

Unfortunately, too many companies wait for a crisis before acting. The result? Crisis hiring, reactive reorganizations, and short-term cost-cutting that compromise long-term capability. A forward-looking HCIS allows organizations to shift from reaction to readiness, building systems that anticipate needs, allocate talent strategically, and support business continuity under any condition.

Investing in people is not an overhead cost but a strategic advantage. Like any sound investment strategy, it demands foresight, data-driven insights, and long-term commitment. By embedding human capital strategy into the core of business planning, companies can weather disruption, seize opportunity, and unlock the full potential of their workforce.

With this foundational perspective in place,
WE NOW TURN TO STEP TWO: ASSESS PORTFOLIO, WHERE WE WILL MAP, MEASURE, AND PRIORITIZE THE ASSETS THAT WILL FUEL FUTURE GROWTH.

IMPLEMENTING
STEP ONE

I. OVERVIEW & OBJECTIVES

- **Objective**

  Develop an HCIS Pro Forma—a strategic, structured framework that aligns workforce planning with business strategy, macroeconomic trends, and operational goals.

- **Key Message**

  Human capital is not a cost to be managed; it is an asset to be optimized. Just as investors use pro forma statements to plan and project financial performance, business leaders must create human capital pro forma statements to forecast and guide human capital investment decisions.

II. STEP-BY-STEP ACTION PLAN

1. Reframe Human Capital as an Investment Asset

- **Actions**

  — Shift the language from labor cost to workforce capital.

  — Emphasize human capital as the only appreciating, renewable asset that directly fuels enterprise value.

— Introduce investment terminology to leadership: yield, volatility, concentration risk, portfolio diversification.

- **Key Message**
  The most enduring returns come from the compounding performance of strategically cultivated human capital, not from fixed assets or short-term efficiency gains.

2. Conduct an Economic & Labor Market Scan

- **Macroeconomic Indicators**
  Gather data on trends that influence labor markets and workforce dynamics:

  — GDP growth, inflation, and interest rates

  — Labor force participation and unemployment

  — Consumer behavior shifts and global supply chain disruptions

  — Legislation or policy changes affecting talent (e.g., visa laws, wage mandates)

  — Technological disruption (e.g., AI adoption, automation)

- **Microeconomic Considerations**

  — Industry-specific pressures (e.g., cost of capital, margin compression)

  — Competitor hiring trends and wage benchmarks

— Shifts in customer preferences or business models

3. Define Organizational Strategic Goals

- **Short-Term (1–2 Years)**
  Examples: Increase market share by 10%, reduce cycle time by 15%, launch new product line, improve customer experience scores

- **Long-Term (3–5+ Years)**
  Examples: Enter new markets, double revenue, prepare for IPO, achieve vertical integration, expand through acquisition

- **Tip**
  Link every workforce strategy to a business objective—human capital should have a defined ROI aligned to organizational priorities.

4. Identify Human Capital Requirements for Each Goal

- **Actions**
  - Deconstruct business goals into required roles, capabilities, and skills.
  - Identify talent gaps, capacity shortfalls, or misaligned team structures.
  - Prioritize high-impact roles (i.e., those directly influencing revenue, innovation, or risk mitigation).

- **Tools & Inputs**
  - Performance data
  - Retention and turnover analytics
  - Employee engagement surveys
  - External brand perception (e.g., Glassdoor)
  - Collaboration with business and HR leaders

5. Conduct a Human Capital SWOT Analysis

- **Strengths**
  Examples: Strong employment brand, high tenure in key roles, robust leadership bench

- **Weaknesses**
  Examples: Lack of role clarity, turnover hotspots, underinvestment in development

- **Opportunities**
  Examples: Access to new graduate pipelines, remote workforce expansion

- **Threats**
  Examples: Talent shortages, wage inflation, skills obsolescence, key person risk

- **Data Sources**
  Examples: Employee feedback platforms, exit interview trends, compensation benchmarks

6. Build the Pro Forma Template

Organize insights into a structured view that connects market data, organizational goals, and

workforce implications. Available at
www.cynthiabentzenmercer.com/resources

III. TOOLS
www.cynthiabentzenmercer.com/resources

- Human Capital Investment Strategy Framework
- HCIS Pro Forma

IV. NEXT STEP
With the HCIS Pro Forma established, proceed to Step Two: Assess Portfolio. This next phase assesses your current workforce's performance and potential against the strategic requirements identified in the pro forma.

STEP TWO

ASSESS PORTFOLIO

An Accounting of Human Capital is the balance sheet of the most valuable assets.

When my son Jacob was about eight years old, he climbed into my lap after school one day, full of excitement about a discovery he had made.

"Mom," he announced, "I'm right-brained."

This caught me off guard. Brain lateralization is not exactly standard content for third graders. Intrigued, I asked how he figured that out. Without hesitation, he pulled a wrinkled quiz from his backpack and handed it to me like evidence in a court case.

As I began reading the questions, I had to stifle a laugh. The quiz was clearly designed for adults—questions like "Do you prefer conceptual thinking over linear logic?" and "Do you often get hunches?" are not exactly questions your average eight-year-old would relate to.

Still amused, I asked, "Jacob, do you know what a hunch is?"

"Of course!" he said confidently, then immediately hunched his shoulders up to his ears like a little turtle, as if to shrug.

It was hilarious—and oddly revealing. What Jacob mistook for a hunch is not so different from how many leaders operate in the workplace.

When it comes to selecting, developing, evaluating, and investing in people's human capital, many leaders rely on the same logic Jacob used: personal interpretations, limited context, and good old-fashioned guesswork. We treat human capital decisions based on hunches.

··

GUT INSTINCT DRIVES MOST OF THE DECISIONS REGARDING HUMAN CAPITAL

—arguably one of an organization's most costly and valuable assets.

For most businesses, **labor is the most significant operating expense**, accounting for 40%–60% of total costs. In retail and manufacturing, labor costs rank second only to the cost of goods sold. Payroll alone typically represents 25%–35% of total revenue, with benefits adding another 25%–40%.

Like financial investments, the returns on human capital can compound over time, yielding significant advantages that foster competitive positioning and market leadership. However, unlike financial assets, which can be acquired and maintained, human capital requires a more nuanced approach emphasizing intentional, strategic investment, continuous development, and effective risk management.

There are various ways to manage one's financial investments. For some, it begins with self-directed investing, where they allocate percentages of their funds to a company-managed portfolio. Depending on their knowledge and confidence, returns can vary. Others opt for computer-generated advisors, which allocate funds based on an algorithm that uses a predefined retirement date and risk profile. Most turn to a financial advisor for support as their investments grow and opportunities for gain or loss increase.

Consider the same analogy for investing in human capital. A company with fewer employees can manage its investment strategy more easily and has closer insight into all its assets than a company with over 5,000 employees. Unfortunately, as organizations grow, they often fail to recognize that the stakes are higher and the potential for gain or loss increases.

Just as a financial advisor is trusted to analyze the performance of your investments and recommend what to remove, add, or double down on, leaders must apply the same rigor when evaluating their HCP.

Businesses can enhance their leadership, innovation, and overall organizational performance by viewing human capital as an investment that requires nurturing, strategic allocation, and regular assessment. Step Two begins with the predictive insight required to assess the health of an HCP and then outlines the step-by-step Accounting of Human Capital (AHC) process.

HUMAN CAPITAL *Attributes*

Just as criteria are used to assess the performance of financial investments, attributes exist for evaluating human capital—namely,

will, ability, ethos, knowledge, skills, and natural talent. As each definition and its relative significance are explored below, remember that those contributing their human capital to work also evaluate the organization and position based on the value they receive in return.

Human Capital Attributes

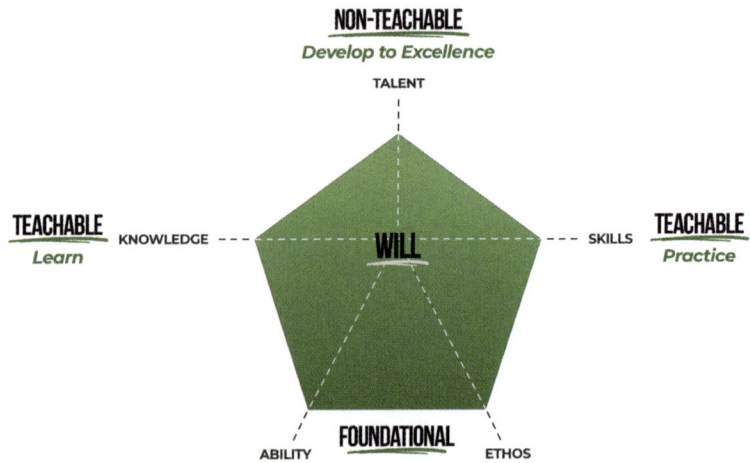

INDIVIDUAL AGENCY

At the heart of every human capital decision lies a powerful, often underestimated force: individual agency. Unlike fixed assets, people are not passive resources to be allocated; they are active agents who choose when, how, and where to contribute their potential. This agency—the capacity to act with intention, autonomy, and alignment—makes human capital fundamentally different from financial capital. It also makes it more valuable.

Every person brings a unique combination of **knowledge, skill, and natural talent.** While knowledge and skill can be assessed and taught, and natural talent can be developed, **will** must be freely given. It cannot be commanded or assumed; it must be inspired.

Will:

The motivation, desire, and personal commitment an individual brings to their role.

In investment terms, will is akin to the risk tolerance an investor is prepared to commit to, understanding that the investment may require patience and resilience. High-performing organizations recognize that employee engagement is closely tied to this "will" factor. A lack of will often arises not from a deficiency in skill or opportunity, but from a misalignment between individual goals and the organization's vision.

Fostering a culture that aligns personal and professional growth is crucial. Leadership ensures employees feel motivated to bring their best selves to the organization by clearly communicating purpose, offering autonomy, and creating an environment conducive to continuous learning.

Unlike financial assets, individuals can choose when and where to share their human capital.

An individual with strongly aligned human capital attributes for a role may choose not to work for a particular organization or leader. **Regrettable attrition occurs when human capital aligns strongly, yet the individual's willingness to contribute to the organization remains low.**

FOUNDATIONAL HUMAN CAPITAL ATTRIBUTES

The foundation of human capital is the ability to perform the job's functions and compatibility with the organization's ethos. Often referred to as "tickets to admission," these attributes are generally based on minimum standards and are expected on day one of employment.

Requisite Ability:
The ability to perform the essential functions of a job.

Requisite ability encompasses the mental and physical capacities necessary to fulfill the responsibilities of a given role. This includes cognitive skills, problem-solving capabilities, memory recall, reasoning, and physical competencies such as strength, coordination, and endurance. However, the way in which organizations define and measure ability has evolved significantly over time, often due to shifting workforce demographics, technological advancements, and increased awareness of biases in selection processes.

Cognitive Ability:
From the early 1900s to the late 1990s, research widely held that general mental ability (GMA) was the most valid predictor of future job performance. A meta-analysis by Hunter & Hunter (1998) found a correlation coefficient of $r = 0.51$ between GMA and job performance, leading companies to adopt cognitive ability tests as a standard selection tool. However, as workforce diversity increased and became larger, more representative studies were conducted, and significant flaws and biases in early assessments were revealed. For example, cognitive ability tests were initially developed and validated on predominantly White male subjects.

When these tests were later used to assess women and Black candidates, they showed an adverse impact, disproportionately screening out individuals from historically underrepresented groups. Adjustments for range restriction reduced the predictive validity of GMA as a selection tool. A 2020 study by Sackett et al. found that the correlation between GMA and performance dropped from $r = 0.51$ to $r = 0.36$ when these adjustments were made.

Today, technology has reduced reliance on cognitive recall. Many tasks that previously required extensive memorization and pattern recognition are now aided by automation and artificial intelligence, making job-specific knowledge tests (with a correlation of .40 with job success) a more relevant selection tool in some instances.

These findings underscore the importance of taking a nuanced approach to assessing mental ability, rather than relying solely on cognitive testing.

Physical Ability:

Physical abilities, such as lifting, endurance, and dexterity, are important factors in defining certain job requirements, like housekeeper, delivery driver, and firefighter. However, the passage of the Americans with Disabilities Act (ADA) in 1990 challenged organizations to rethink how they assess and define physical ability.

Before the ADA, hiring decisions often incorporated assumptions about an individual's capacity based on visible or perceived disabilities. These assumptions resulted in the systemic exclusion of capable candidates. The ADA prohibits such practices, requiring employers to focus on job-related performance rather than preconceived notions of ability.

Key considerations for requiring physical ability in an equitable and compliant manner include:

- **Ensuring requirements are essential.** Physical ability tests should align directly with tasks essential for job performance. Employers must avoid unnecessary physical criteria that could unintentionally exclude qualified individuals.

- **Providing reasonable accommodation.** The ADA requires employers to modify work environments or responsibilities to enable individuals with disabilities to perform their roles effectively.

- **Reframing physical ability through a performance lens.** Instead of assuming that a disability prevents a person from performing a task, organizations must assess how a candidate or employee performs with reasonable accommodation.

Neurodiversity:

As awareness of neurodiversity has grown, organizations have begun rethinking how they define ability and assess talent. Neurodivergent individuals, including those with autism, ADHD, dyslexia, and other cognitive differences, often bring exceptional strengths in problem-solving, creativity, pattern recognition, and deep-focus thinking. Organizations that fail to account for neurodiversity risk overlooking top-tier talent because their evaluation criteria favor neurotypical thinking styles.

However, traditional selection processes may inadvertently disadvantage neurodivergent candidates with limited prediction of future performance:

- **Overreliance on Unstructured Verbal Interviews:** Standard, verbal interviews often emphasize quick verbal responses, eye contact, and social fluency—criteria that may not correlate with job performance for neurodivergent individuals. This will be discussed further in Step Five. Unstructured interviews have a weak predictive validity, with a correlation coefficient of $r = 0.22$.

- **Personality-Based Unstructured Interviews:** These

can often emphasize leadership potential through extroverted traits, which can unfairly disadvantage neurodivergent individuals who may be highly competent but less outwardly expressive. Extroversion has a weak predictive validity, with a correlation coefficient of $r = 0.11$.

- **Rigid Cognitive Assessments:** Timed logic and reasoning tests often measure how quickly someone arrives at an answer rather than how well they think through a problem. Many neurodivergent individuals excel in deep analysis but may require more time to process information. Cognitive ability assessments have a weak-to-moderate predictive validity, with a correlation coefficient of $r = 0.36$.

How we define ability has profound implications for how organizations attract, retain, and develop talent. By applying rigorous yet inclusive evaluation methods, organizations can build more diverse, high-performing teams—not by lowering standards, but by expanding how they recognize and measure excellence.

Ethos:
The shared norms, guiding principles, values, and attitudes of an organization, actualized by who they select, develop, and promote.

Every organization has a unique ethos, but ethos is not defined by plaques on the wall or words in a handbook. It is actualized by where the company invests. Whether explicitly stated or subtly expressed, company ethos becomes visible in the behaviors that are reinforced, the people who are elevated, and the decisions that are made when no one is watching.

Faith-based institutions may prioritize spiritual alignment and comfort with prayer in the workplace. The U.S. Marine Corps attracts individuals who embody tradition, honor, and resilience. Southwest Airlines seeks individuals who lead with humor, courage, and compassion. These are not just cultural quirks; they are strategic choices that protect and perpetuate organizational DNA.

Nevertheless, for ethos to become a strategic asset, it must be intentionally integrated into human capital investment decisions, beginning with the selection process.

Culture Fit vs. Cultural Contribution:

Organizations often talk about hiring for "culture fit," but when misapplied, this term can unintentionally lead to homogeneity and exclusion. Instead, companies should aim to select for cultural alignment, seeking individuals whose behaviors and values resonate with the company's ethos while also honoring authenticity and welcoming difference.

To achieve this, consider incorporating ethos-based prompts and structured questions into the selection process:

"Tell me about a time you had to uphold a team value under pressure."

"What role does fun/respect/faith/tradition (tailored to company ethos) play in your ideal work environment?"

"Describe the kind of culture where you thrive—what norms and attitudes bring out your best?"

These questions are not about excluding difference—they are about uncovering behavioral alignment without compromising diversity of identity, thought, and perspective.

Why It Matters: Organizational Stability and Scalability:

A well-articulated ethos becomes a stabilizing force, particularly during periods of growth, disruption, or leadership transitions. When individuals across the HCP are aligned in their approach to work, decision-making, and leadership, the organization scales with greater cohesion, trust, and efficiency. In contrast, when value misalignment permeates the workforce, it breeds confusion, erodes trust, and increases turnover.

Ethos is also the invisible glue that holds strategy and execution together. You can have the right business plan, the right systems, and the right markets—but if the people executing it do not believe in what the organization stands for, the plan collapses. When aligned across the organization, it drives performance, engagement, and reputation. The most enduring companies do not just have great strategies—they have people who have a shared sense of mission and demonstrate it in their daily actions.

THE QUICKEST WAY TO ERODE CULTURE AND DIMINISH EMPLOYEE ENGAGEMENT IS WHEN LEADERS BEHAVE INCONSISTENTLY WITH THE MISSION STATEMENT POSTED IN THE LOBBY.

TEACHABLE

A critical yet often overlooked distinction in workforce strategy is the difference between what can be taught and what cannot be taught. This understanding sits at the heart of every human capital decision, from selecting and onboarding to succession planning and leadership development. It determines how companies invest in their people, define success in different roles, and balance training costs with the imperative to attract and retain the right talent.

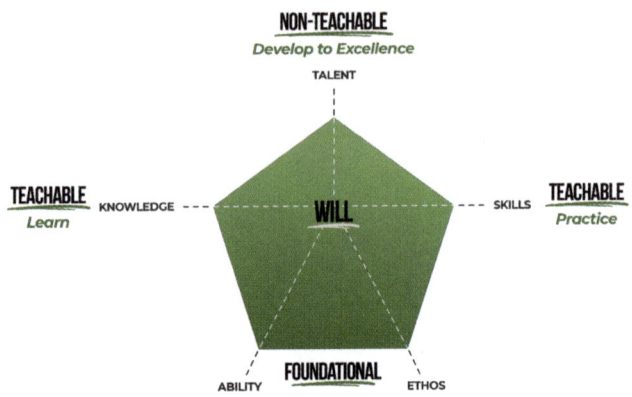

At its core, something teachable presumes that the individual has the foundational cognitive or physical ability to learn and apply it. Basic teachable competencies—like typing, using spreadsheet software, or reading a profit and loss statement—are transferable across industries. More specialized, technical skills—such as dealing blackjack or performing ultrasounds—are unique to specific professions but can still be developed through education and practice. In contrast, other attributes remain stubbornly resistant to training, regardless of an organization's effort. Some aspects of performance are deeply ingrained, embedded in an individual's natural wiring and unlikely to be meaningfully changed.

Understanding these differences is not just an academic exercise but a business imperative. Organizations frequently miscalculate what can be developed and where natural ability is the decisive factor. The consequences of these misjudgments ripple through hiring processes, leadership pipelines, and employee retention rates.

Companies that invest in upskilling employees see measurable returns. Studies have shown that organizations with robust learning and development initiatives generate significantly higher revenue per employee and have stronger retention rates than those that neglect workforce education. The ability to teach is an asset, but it must be applied strategically. Teachable human capital attributes include knowledge and skill.

Knowledge:
The information and understanding we acquire through education or experience.

Knowledge forms the foundation of teachability. It comprises facts, principles, and conceptual frameworks that can be acquired through formal education, training, and practical experience. In many ways, it is the easiest piece of the puzzle. Most people can learn the steps in a process, the elements of a strategy, or the mechanics of an industry. For example, a bartender knows the ingredients in a specialty cocktail, and a mail carrier has memorized the delivery route. As noted in Step One, the dependency of individuals to attain rote job knowledge has diminished with the availability of Meta, ChatGPT, search engines, and automation.

Skills:
Skills are the demonstrated ability to apply knowledge in real-world situations.

Skills are capabilities acquired through learning, refined through experience, and demonstrated through effective execution. They require instruction, practice, feedback, and time. A person may understand the theory of sales, but until they can handle live objections and close deals in unpredictable conditions, they have not yet mastered the *skill* of selling. Likewise, a medical student may memorize every surgical step.

However, the *skill* of surgery only emerges when they can apply that knowledge with precision in a high-stakes environment.

In short, skills are what transform knowledge into action. They are observable, teachable, and—when cultivated intentionally—scalable across teams and organizations.

NON-TEACHABLE

Not everything can be taught. Decades of behavioral science and psychology studies have demonstrated that while people can improve in many areas, innate strengths provide an undeniable advantage. Traits such as analytical reasoning, pattern recognition, or interpersonal charisma are complex and inherent to an individual's makeup. While they can be honed, they cannot be installed.

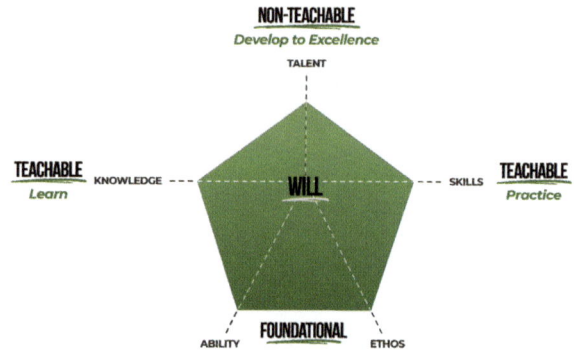

Talent:
Consistency of thoughts, feelings, and behaviors, along with innate aptitude that comes naturally without effort and can be developed to near-perfect performance.

Throughout this book, the term "talent" includes what the research community generally refers to as personality traits. Unlike knowledge and skills, which can be acquired and refined, talent is intrinsic. It is an individual's natural disposition toward specific ways of thinking, processing information, and responding to the world. It is what a person does effortlessly, the areas where they show early aptitude and rapid development with minimal instruction.

Historically, businesses have struggled with the concept of talent. In domains such as sports, music, or art, natural talent is often readily apparent, as evidenced by speed, accuracy, or creative brilliance. However, it often goes unnoticed in corporate environments or is overshadowed by more easily quantifiable factors, such as credentials and experience.

Organizations often assume that anyone can be trained to excellence, failing to recognize that while most people can become competent with sufficient effort, few will achieve true mastery without an underlying talent. Too often, leaders waste time trying to coach individuals to materially improve in areas that do not come naturally.

In reviewing the examples, remember that a natural talent can be developed to near-perfect performance, while a softer area can be marginally improved or mitigated. As Einstein said, "Everyone is a genius. But if you judge a fish by its ability to climb a tree, it will live its whole life believing it is stupid."

Examples of Natural Talent:

- **Creativity**: The ability to generate novel and productive ideas.
- **Curiosity**: A strong desire to explore and discover.
- **Hope**: Optimism about the future.
- **Humor**: The ability to bring smiles and find joy.

- **Judgment**: Critical thinking and seeing all sides of an issue.

- **Leadership**: Inspiring and guiding others.

- **Love of Learning**: A passion for acquiring new knowledge.

- **Perspective**: The ability to provide wise counsel and see the bigger picture.

- **Perseverance**: Persistence in overcoming obstacles.

- **Prudence**: Cautiousness in decision-making.

- **Self-Regulation**: Managing one's emotions and behaviors effectively.

- **Social Intelligence**: Understanding and navigating social situations effectively.

- **Teamwork**: Working well within a group.

- **Zest**: Approaching life with excitement and energy.

Some of the most pervasive hiring and development mistakes arise from failing to acknowledge these realities. Companies invest heavily in training programs to address what are, at their core, talent mismatches. They promote employees based on tenure and technical proficiency, only to discover that leadership success requires a separate, largely unteachable set of attributes—such as emotional intelligence, adaptability, and executive presence. They overlook individuals with high potential who do not fit traditional molds, missing out on exceptional talent because it does not manifest in expected ways.

Consider Susan Boyle for instance. When she first stepped onto the stage of *Britain's Got Talent* in 2009, the audience and judges exchanged skeptical glances. Her unassuming presence and slightly awkward demeanor did not fit the typical mold of a superstar. Many quietly dismissed her even before she could open her mouth. However, the moment she began to sing "I Dreamed a Dream," the atmosphere in the room transformed. Her rich, powerful, and deeply emotive voice shattered every assumption. She immediately demonstrated that true talent is not always packaged in the way people expect.

Though her voice was naturally extraordinary, she learned from professional coaching to enhance her stage presence, refine her technique, and build confidence in the spotlight. With guidance, she acquired the knowledge and skills to navigate the music industry and improve her craft, propelling her career forward. Susan's story is a testament to not allowing the teachable deficiencies to overshadow the raw talent that can be developed.

How many Susan Boyles are overlooked in the workplace due to knowledge and skill deficiencies or non-predictive characteristics?

THE IMPLICATIONS FOR ORGANIZATIONS ARE PROFOUND.

Selecting, developing, and succession planning must consider the interplay between teachable and non-teachable attributes. The cost of training varies widely. Some skills require only brief instruction, while others demand years of deliberate practice and repetition. Organizations must decide whether to select someone with an existing capability or develop it internally, considering which approach is more effective. Time, resources, and the complexity of the skill all contribute to that calculation.

When selecting, organizations should prioritize talent in roles where skills can be developed and enhanced. A naturally gifted problem-solver can be taught to excel in financial modeling, and a charismatic and emotionally intelligent individual can learn sales techniques. However, the reverse is far less feasible—no amount of training will turn someone into a natural smiler or transform an individual without strategic thinking ability into a visionary strategist.

The same principle applies to internal development. Investing in skill development for employees with strong innate aptitudes is a high-return strategy. However, **spending years molding someone into a fundamentally unsuited role is costly.** Leaders must understand the difference between growth potential and futility.

Moreover, this distinction is critical in succession planning. **Too often, leadership pipelines are built around experience and tenure rather than true leadership talent.** The assumption that a long-serving, technically proficient manager will automatically transition into a great executive is one of the most common—and damaging—miscalculations in business. Organizations that fail to assess leadership readiness through the lens of natural talent risk elevating individuals who will struggle, stagnate, and ultimately fail.

THE PARADIGM SHIFT

It may feel that the subject of knowledge, skills, and natural talent has been thoroughly reviewed, and any further discussion would be redundant. However, getting this right is the most crucial factor in realizing the full potential of the HCIS. Furthermore, it is the least understood differentiation within businesses worldwide. Even when leaders begin to have a light bulb moment, societal norms, traditional points of view, and data collection continually reinforce the old paradigm.

Future of Jobs Report

In an era defined by technological acceleration, it's tempting to believe that skill development alone can future-proof our workforce or that technology alone will solve the labor shortage. Yet the *2025 Future of Jobs Report* offers critical insight that challenges this assumption.

Among the top ten of the 26 "skills" identified as increasing, decreasing, or remaining stable in demand: *creative thinking, resilience, flexibility and agility, curiosity and lifelong learning, leadership and social influence, talent management, and analytical thinking.* However, by our definition, these are not "skills." They are natural talents.

Skills on the Rise, 2025–2030

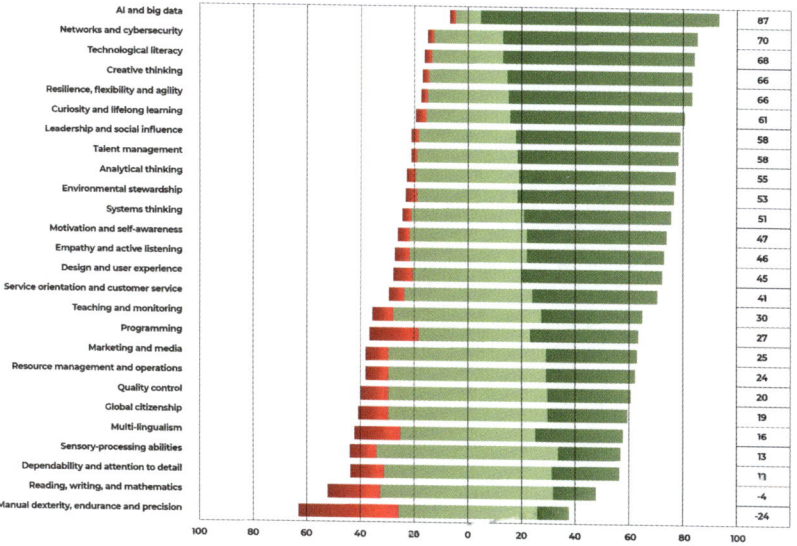

SHARE OF EMPLOYEES SURVEYED (%)

Source: World Economic Forum, Future of Jobs Survey 2024.

This distinction matters. Unlike software proficiencies or process knowledge, which can be trained in structured environments, these traits are inherent capacities, differentiators that emerge early and develop with experience, not instruction. Yet in many organizations, human capital strategy still treats these qualities as if they can be built from scratch. We confuse potential with proficiency, overlooking the predictive power of innate wiring. That is not just a misstep. In today's climate, it is a strategic liability.

The HCIS provides a significant competitive advantage because corporate America still operates with outdated, non-predictive talent strategies. The challenge is building leadership literacy and maintaining discipline even when it feels counterintuitive or not widely reinforced by your competitors.

Understanding what can and cannot be taught is a competitive advantage. Organizations that make strategic human capital decisions, select talent, develop knowledge and skills, and align individuals with their innate strengths create a more capable, engaged, productive, and resilient workforce. We will not AI our way out of a labor shortage!

NO MATTER HOW MANY RESOURCES A COMPANY INVESTS IN TRAINING, SOME THINGS WILL NEVER BE LEARNED.

Moreover, a business's best investment is ensuring it never tries to teach what should be selected.

Executing ALL HUMAN CAPITAL ATTRIBUTES

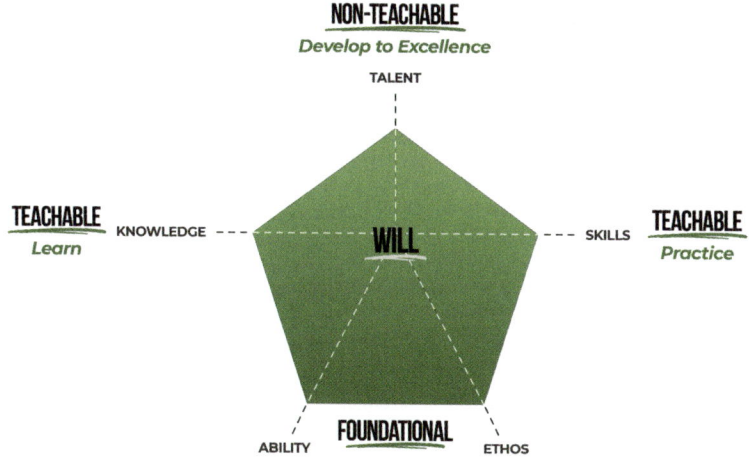

NON-TEACHABLE
Develop to Excellence
TALENT

TEACHABLE
Learn
KNOWLEDGE

WILL

SKILLS
TEACHABLE
Practice

FOUNDATIONAL
ABILITY   ETHOS

As leaders begin to fully understand the separate human capital attributes, it can be difficult to discern them individually and visualize them all working in concert. As a proud aunt of a Marine, I have come to appreciate that one of the most esteemed roles in the United States Marine Corps vividly illustrates every element of human capital executed flawlessly—the Marine Body Bearers. Consider the following illustration.

Tasked with carrying the caskets of fallen Marines, presidents, and dignitaries, Marine Body Bearers' silent precision embodies the highest physical and mental endurance standards. While the role may appear simple—lifting and carrying a casket—it requires an extraordinary combination of strength, skill, and an unwavering commitment to excellence.

Before a Marine is identified as a candidate for Body Bearer, they are vetted based on the two foundational attributes of human capital: **ethos and ability**. This very elite group of men must uphold and live up to the values of the Marine Corps and the sanctity of the Body Bearers' mission. They must also meet the significant physical ability criteria.

The ceremonial casket, adorned with the American flag, can weigh over 800 pounds when occupied. Only six Marines lift and precisely carry this weight, often holding it at shoulder height for extended periods while ascending the marble steps of Arlington National Cemetery or maneuvering through historic churches. Candidates for the Body Bearers must be 70–76 inches tall and possess exceptional raw strength, with the ability to deadlift over 400 pounds and sustain high endurance levels under rigorous physical conditions. The physical ability requirement highlights an extreme example. However, strength alone is insufficient.

The Marines must possess profound **knowledge**—an understanding of the weight they bear, both literal and symbolic. Body Bearers study the traditions of the Marine Corps, the significance of military honors, the rich history of those they serve, and the precise cadence and ceremonial steps. This awareness instills a sense of duty that transcends mere performance, transforming into a calling.

The role demands acute technical **skills**. Every movement is rehearsed to ensure absolute uniformity—the team steps in unison, pivots with precision, and silently lowers the casket. The grip on the casket must be perfectly coordinated to prevent any shifting, and each Marine must anticipate the movements of the others without hesitation. One mistake—one falter—can disrupt the sacred ceremony, representing an unacceptable failure in their solemn duty.

The training is brutal. Candidates undergo months of instruction in weightlifting, marching, and drill maneuvers. They train in silence, honing their ability to communicate through unspoken cues. They rehearse under varying conditions—on uneven ground and in inclement weather—until their actions become second nature.

Beyond physical ability, knowledge, and technical skill, the role demands an **inherent talent**—an understanding of reverence, discipline, and composure. The mental fortitude required is immense. There is no room for distraction and no space for error. These Marines are entrusted with honoring the fallen and representing the entire Marine Corps. Every movement is a tribute; every step is a demonstration of respect. This level of responsibility demands a distinctive combination of emotional intelligence and professionalism.

Each soldier is meticulously sourced, carefully selected, thoroughly trained, and skillfully developed. Still, the role of a Body Bearer requires **will**. While the men are selected as candidates based on their ethos and physicality, the intensity of training, which involves building physical ability and the pressure to execute knowledge and skills with perfection, requires a significant commitment. Only a few Marines will ever wear the title of Body Bearer.

While most of the roles within an organization's HCP do not bear the literal or figurative weight of the Marine Body Bearers, the individual and collective components of human capital remain critical. When human capital is strategically placed, it acts as a force multiplier of performance by amplifying an organization's ability to generate value beyond the sum of its individual contributors.

Force MULTIPLIERS

High-performing employees not only complete tasks but also innovate, optimize, and create efficiencies that drive exponential returns. This is particularly evident in economies of scale, where increased productivity per employee results in lower marginal costs as an organization expands. For example, experienced employees refine processes, automate repetitive tasks, and mentor others in knowledge-based industries, compounding efficiency gains over time. Using our early example, where all other military branches have eight body bearers, the combined human capital attributes required of the Marine Corps allows them to only deploy six.

Beyond driving growth, human capital also plays a critical role in absorbing economic downturns. Unlike fixed costs, such as infrastructure or inventory, an agile workforce can pivot strategies, innovate in response to challenges, and maintain operational continuity even in periods of uncertainty. We saw this come to life in the Joplin example, and many organizations experienced this firsthand during the COVID-19 pandemic.

During downturns, organizations with highly aligned human capital are better positioned to reallocate talent, optimize workflows, and retain institutional knowledge, reducing the disruptive impact of layoffs or restructuring. Research from the World Economic Forum suggests that companies prioritizing workforce adaptability recover more quickly from economic shocks, as employees with broad skill sets can be redeployed across various functions, thereby minimizing inefficiencies and lost productivity.

BY THE NUMBERS

According to a study by researchers at Indiana University, involving over 600,000 people across various job types, industries, time periods, and assessment methods, **top-performing individuals deliver 400% greater productivity than those with average performance.** Read that again! This is where HCIS delivers the greatest return. Investing in developing skills and knowledge in individuals with strong talent potential will yield a significant return.

One of the most compelling ways to demonstrate the return on investment of human capital is to mathematically quantify the performance gap between top performers and the average workforce. By calculating **output as a percentage of the median performer's output,** organizations can see, with hard numbers, how much more value superior contributors bring to the table.

The formula is simple:

(Individual Output ÷ Output at the 50th Percentile) × 100 = Percentage of Output Relative to Average

This approach is grounded in decades of performance research. According to Hunter, Schmidt, and Judiesch (1990), the standard deviation of output—a common statistical measure of variability—increases with job complexity. This means that the performance gap between top and average performers is significantly wider in leadership and professional roles than in routine or semi-skilled jobs.

Using the 84th percentile (one standard deviation above the mean) as our benchmark for "superior performance," the results are telling:

The Percentage Output Above the Average Performer Generated by Superior Performance

Semi-Skilled Worker	**19%**
Skilled Worker	**32%**
Manager/Professional	**48%**

Example in Practice:

Imagine a mid-sized manufacturing company with 50 skilled technicians on the production floor. If the average technician produces $100,000 in annual value, a technician operating at the 84th percentile contributes $132,000—$32,000 more each year. Now, multiply that by just 10 high performers, and you are looking at an additional $320,000 in output annually, **without increasing headcount.**

Now apply the same math to leadership roles. A manager at the 84th percentile is delivering 48% more output than their average counterpart. If the average value of a mid-level manager's output is $100,000, then a top-performing manager generates $148,000. Multiply that across a team of five such leaders, and the financial advantage grows exponentially. **Ultimately, fewer people can produce the same amount of output.**

Depending on the type of positions within your organization and its relative size, the percentage of output from top-performing individuals versus average-performing individuals represents a significant opportunity for financial return.

A complementary measure is the **dollar value of output** across a normal distribution. Let's say your organization estimates the average output per employee at $100,000. Using a conservative 40% standard deviation model:

Dollar Value of Output

16th Percentile	50th Percentile	84th Percentile
$60,000	$100,000	$140,000

This means that a single high performer can be worth as

much as two low performers combined. That's not just a performance gap—it's a strategic opportunity for optimization.

Example in Practice:

Consider a professional services firm with 100 employees. If 20 of those are operating at the 84th percentile ($140,000 output) and the rest are at the median ($100,000), the total output is:

$(20 \times \$140,000) + (80 \times \$100,000) = \$2.8$ million $+ \$8$ million $= \textbf{\$10.8 million}$

Now, imagine raising just 10 more employees from the 50th to the 84th percentile. That alone would increase output by another $400,000 annually.

This is the math behind the message. Even modest increases in the number of top performers—or retaining high performers who might otherwise leave—can have a multimillion-dollar impact over time. Conversely, tolerating consistent underperformance or failing to invest in development leads to compounded losses.

When quantifying the impact of every individual positioned to work at the top of their human capital, with joy and engagement, we recognize that **even minor improvements in the number of top-performing individuals can have an exponential financial impact.**

···

Accounting OF HUMAN CAPITAL: CURRENT ROLE

To treat human capital as an investment, organizations must

learn to account for it in financial terms. This is where the concept of AHC comes into play. Much like an investor tracks the performance of their portfolio, companies must monitor the performance and potential of their human capital. Perhaps the most significant business case for conducting an AHC is the return on investment in human capital.

As established, every person brings human capital to their role. When all individuals are aggregated, this represents an organization's HCP. Just as each Marine Corps Body Bearer is individually evaluated among every element of the human capital attributes so that the team executes flawlessly, organizations must employ the same rigor to every position within their HCP.

Depending on a company's size and complexity, this portfolio evaluation can be rigorous and time-consuming, which is often why competitors overlook it. However, it is essential to cultivate potential and gain a strategic advantage.

The AHC involves an assessment of every individual's human capital, segmented by **current performance and talent for the role.** While a company-wide AHC is ideal, the priority should begin with the organization's top two to three tiers, as these significantly influence driving culture and results.

PERFORMANCE

The AHC is illustrated on a four-quadrant matrix. Performance is represented on the y-axis, ranging from soft (bottom left) to strong (top left). The organization's performance assessment should objectively rate the individual's knowledge, skills, and outcomes. The rating must focus on the teachable elements of the role and the associated results. The goal is to gather as many objective criteria as possible to inform an overall performance rating.

While most companies employ a structured approach to performance evaluation, several additional suggestions are outlined in the implementation guide at the end of this step. Recognizing that much of the performance data collected encompasses varying degrees of subjectivity, using a diverse range of information can improve the accuracy of the assessment.

It is recommended that the organization utilize the appropriate performance measures for its environment, keeping in mind that objectivity is crucial. If an organization uses its standard performance appraisal to rate performance, care should be taken to remove non-teachable, talent-related attributes, as these are measured separately, as discussed below. The y-axis can be adapted to use the organization's standard performance rating scale, e.g., 1 – 4.

AHC Performance/Talent Matrix

4	**STRONG PERFORMANCE** <u>Soft</u> Talent for Role	**STRONG PERFORMANCE** **STRONG TALENT FOR ROLE**
3		
2	<u>Soft</u> Performance <u>Soft</u> Talent for Role	<u>Soft</u> Performance **STRONG TALENT FOR ROLE**
1		

CURRENT PERFORMANCE

TALENT FOR CURRENT ROLE

Source: Copyright 2023, Talent Plus®, Lincoln, Nebraska.

TALENT FOR ROLE

Talent for a role is represented on the x-axis from soft (bottom left) to strong (bottom right). Assessing talent for a role focuses on the non-teachable yet developable aspects. While performance indicates what the individual does, talent represents how they achieve the outcomes. If an organization has defined leadership competencies or other non-teachable position expectations, these should be incorporated into assessing talent for the role.

There are several ways to assess the non-teachable talent for a role, depending on the time and level of financial commitment you are willing to make. Because the initial AHC is an exercise of assessing the incumbent's talent in a current role, a less predictive yet directionally helpful approach is outlined first. However, using a validated assessment is always the recommended approach. This will be discussed further later in this step.

ACES

When a leader has direct oversight and observational insights of an incumbent, the ACES model can help to assess an individual's natural talent for a role (Bentzen-Mercer & Rath, 2024). The leader is encouraged to consider the non-teachable primary functions of the position:

- **Affirmation:**
  Do the position's primary responsibilities bring them intrinsic satisfaction and joy? For example, when performing at an excellent level, the individual feels energized rather than drained.

- **Consistency:**
  Does the individual consistently exhibit behaviors that deliver excellence? For example, how they show up and perform is not conditional.

- **Excellence:**
  Does the individual consistently perform with excellence, surpassing most others? For example, others seek this person out for help or guidance.

- **Spontaneity:**
  Does the individual naturally think, feel, and behave in a particular way without exerting effort or giving it much thought? For example, the individual's performance is natural, not forced.

All four criteria must be met when assessing natural talent for a role using the ACES model. If any criteria do not apply, it is important to dig deeper. If the incumbent consistently delivers excellence with little effort but finds the role or a particular aspect of the job unfulfilling, it is essential to understand why. It is possible that this is not an area of natural talent, or there may be underlying reasons. However, if two or more criteria are not met, the chances that the individual is in a role not directly aligned with their natural talent are high.

Examples of ACES in action:

RESTAURANT HOSTESS: SOFIA

Affirmation
Sofia lights up when guests walk through the door. Even during high-volume rushes, she smiles genuinely, remembers frequent diners by name, and seems to thrive in the flow of customer interaction. She routinely volunteers to take the front shift because she enjoys being the first face people see.

Consistency
Regardless of whether it's a slow Tuesday lunch or a packed Saturday night, Sofia's demeanor never shifts. Her greetings are warm, she stays attentive, and she maintains composure even when wait times spike.

Her manager never worries about "which Sofia" is showing up.

Excellence
Sofia is frequently requested by name in online reviews. Servers report that guests seated by her are more likely to stay, order more, and rate their experience higher. New hostesses shadow her during onboarding because of her seamless communication with both guests and staff.

Spontaneity
Her spatial awareness and timing appear instinctual. She balances table turnover, server capacity, and customer preferences without hesitation. She anticipates needs before they arise—offering menus, water, or reassurance with ease and without prompting.

HOTEL HOUSEKEEPER: JOHN

Affirmation
John finds genuine satisfaction in creating clean, peaceful environments. He often expresses pride in a job well done and quietly checks that every towel is perfectly folded and every detail in the room is spotless—even when no one's watching.

Consistency
His rooms are always inspection-ready. No matter the shift, floor, or guest type, leaders can rely on John to meet brand standards. He rarely needs coaching or reminders.

Excellence
Guest comment cards often note the "spotless room" or "extra touches," such as a carefully arranged welcome towel. Fellow housekeepers often seek his input when unsure about best practices.

Spontaneity
He does not use checklists as crutches; his rhythm and sequence seem hardwired. He notices stains or missing items with a glance. Tidiness appears to be a fundamental aspect of how he perceives the world.

TEAM LEADER: RONDA

Affirmation
Ronda gains energy from mentoring others. She celebrates wins publicly, and you will often find her staying late, not for deliverables, but to coach a team member through a challenge. Her joy comes from seeing others succeed.

Consistency
Her team describes her as "steady," even under pressure. Her communication is measured, she maintains expectations, and she addresses conflicts directly but respectfully. You will not find Ronda having "off days" that derail the group.

Excellence
Ronda's department consistently meets or exceeds performance goals. High-potential employees request to be transferred to their team. Her peers defer to her in cross-functional projects due to her insightful contributions and team outcomes.

Spontaneity
She instinctively reads people. In meetings, she senses tension before it is verbalized and adjusts tone or strategy with ease. Her feedback is always tailored and timely, even in impromptu conversations.

INTERPRETING THE ACCOUNTING OF HUMAN CAPITAL

Up to this point, it has been established that not everyone is exceptional at everything. There has also been evidence of the force multiplier that exists when the right individual's human capital is cast in the right role. Later, we will focus on the exponential intrinsic satisfaction and motivation that employees experience when working in a role that complements their natural talents. In other words, getting it right is a win/win.

It is essential to acknowledge that most companies have a significant portion of their employees who may not be working in a position that fully aligns with their greatest strengths. According to Gallup's research, a significant portion of employees feel they are not in roles that fully utilize their natural talents. Specifically, Gallup found that **only about 10% of workers possess the natural talent to be effective leaders**, suggesting that many employees are not in positions that align with their inherent strengths.

This is not an indictment on the person; rather, it is an organizational miss. As the AHC is visually illustrated on the four-quadrant matrix, it is vital to remember **the intentional use of "for the role." As stated earlier, the premise is that everyone has talent.** The question is whether their talent is aligned with the role they are currently in.

Position Profile Matrix

Recognizing that talent attributes are non-teachable yet can be developed to near-perfect performance, attention should first be directed to the right side of the AHC model. These individuals represent your *pros* in role (top right quadrant) or *high potentials* in role (bottom right quadrant). *High potentials* are those identified as having strong talent for the role but not yet performing at an excellent level. They require further assessment to determine if they can be coached to become pros within their current position.

AHC Position Profile Matrix

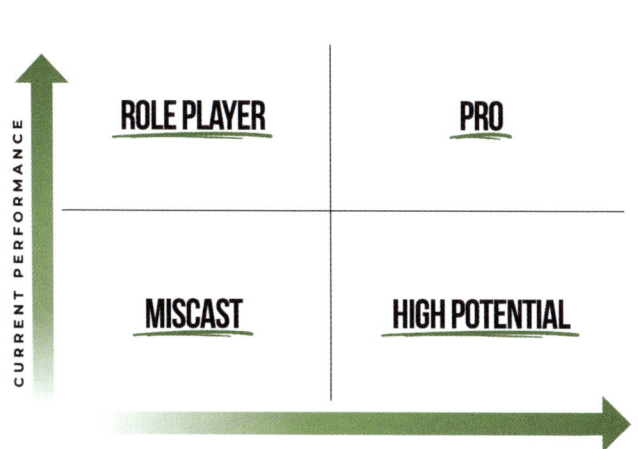

Source: Copyright 2023, Talent Plus®, Lincoln, Nebraska.

The left side of the chart represents role players who demonstrate knowledge, skill, and output; however, they have a softer talent for the role, as indicated by the top left quadrant. Those who are miscast and both underperform and do not demonstrate talent for the role appear in the lower left quadrant.

In a natural distribution, before implementing the HCIS, you might expect 10%–20% in the lower left, 40%–50% in the upper left, 20%–30% in the lower right, and 10%–20% in the upper right. **Companies that have not been using predictive assessments to select and promote employees often find that as many as 70% of the portfolio falls to the left.**

As revealed later in this section, companies that rely on unstructured interviews and intuition, rather than valid predictive assessments, when selecting and promoting employees, create their HCP with weak predictive validity (r = 0.19–0.22). It is therefore unsurprising if a significant talent imbalance is revealed.

A word of caution: If an organization has not used validated selection instruments and finds 70% of the portfolio to the right of the AHC, it may be worthwhile to revalidate the criteria and ratings. This would be an unusual distribution, and inter-rater bias may provide false positive results and underrepresent the work ahead.

THE RESULTS OF THE AHC REPRESENT THE GREATEST OPPORTUNITY TO MOVE THE HCP FROM A LABOR BURDEN TO AN INVESTMENT STRATEGY.

While the initial assessment may cause concern, correcting and rebalancing the portfolio will be outlined in Steps Three through Six.

ASSESSING *Potential*

While evaluating an incumbent's talents for their current role based on past observations is not scientific, it does provide insight into where their natural talents are evident. However, **predicting an individual's *potential* for a *future* role is more complex and carries greater risk and reward.**

Before adding a new fund to a financial portfolio or making a more significant investment, savvy investors conduct thorough research and seek relevant data to inform their decisions and enhance their chances of success. Unfortunately, organizations often rely on non-predictive measures to assess an employee's fitness or readiness for a future role. However, given the time and money at stake, evaluating an individual's talent potential must be approached with statistical rigor.

Until organizations and leaders stop relying on non-predictive measures to gauge future performance, they will not yield a return on their investment in human capital. Every external selection and internal promotional decision hinges on increasing the probability that the individual will deliver exceptional performance.

NON-PREDICTIVE ASSUMPTIONS

In workforce strategy, what feels intuitive is not always what proves predictive. Too often, hiring and promotion decisions are guided by long-held assumptions rather than validated indicators of future success. These biases—rooted in tradition, perception, or convenience—can quietly undermine even the most well-intentioned talent strategies.

The most persistent myths in selection and promotion: that past performance guarantees future readiness, that gender does not affect perceptions of leadership potential, and that age, whether too young or too old, can serve as a proxy for capability. Each assumption distorts decision-making and dilutes the value of a truly optimized HCP. To outperform the market, organizations must confront and replace these shortcuts with evidence-based practices that recognize human capital as both measurable and multidimensional.

PAST PERFORMANCE

Recent research suggests that past performance in a particular role is not a reliable predictor of future success in new roles. However, leaders often emphasize past performance as the sole predictor of an individual's performance in a new position. Across various industries, we observe exceptional bedside nurses being promoted to nursing managers, top-performing salespeople transitioned to sales managers, and outstanding facilitators being elevated to lead a training function.

A study by Egon Zehnder (2024) involving 800 executives worldwide revealed that 78% believe past performance is no longer the best indicator of success in a new role, emphasizing the importance of natural talent instead. The idea that excellence in the current role is automatically transferable to the next role is a shortcut that can lead to costly consequences. The natural talent required for success in the new role may be significantly different and untested.

GENDER

Research involving over 29,000 management-track employees across North America found that, despite receiving higher performance ratings, women were consistently rated lower on potential (MIT Sloan, 2022). Three key conclusions may explain the disconnect between performance and potential.

The first is the persistence of gender stereotypes, which associate leadership with traditionally masculine traits such as assertiveness, dominance, and aggression. This often leads evaluators—consciously or unconsciously—to overlook leadership behaviors more commonly expressed by women, such as collaboration, empathy, and inclusive decision-making. These traits, while critical to modern leadership, are not always valued in promotion discussions, especially when the cultural archetype of a leader remains centered on command-and-control behaviors. As a result, women who lead through influence or consensus may be perceived as less decisive or strategic, which can limit their perceived readiness for advancement.

The second is the conditioning of women to work hard, keep their heads down, and wait to be recognized, concealing their aspirations (Bentzen-Mercer & Rath, 2024). This social conditioning, rooted in early education, workplace dynamics, and cultural expectations, teaches many high-performing women that ambition should be demonstrated through diligence rather than declared through self-promotion. Consequently, they may not vocalize career goals, advocate for stretch roles, or proactively seek sponsorship, all of which are behaviors typically interpreted as indicators of high potential. In performance reviews, this silence can be misinterpreted as a lack of ambition or interest in leadership, perpetuating the gap.

The third is the assumptions often made about a woman's priorities and perceived limitations. Whether explicitly stated or subtly implied, decision-makers may assume a woman will be less committed due to caregiving responsibilities or less mobile due to family considerations. These assumptions—often untested and unspoken—can result in women being "protected" from growth opportunities, high-visibility assignments, or demanding roles. Moreover, these assumptions are rarely made about men, even when they share similar life circumstances, thereby reinforcing an uneven evaluation of potential.

Whatever the reason for the disconnect, changing workforce demographics provides a rich opportunity for companies willing to leverage gender as a human capital strategy.

Key Implications:

- **Leadership Pipeline:** Women are increasingly qualified for leadership, technical, and specialist roles that historically skewed male, reshaping succession planning and talent development strategies.

- **Workforce Dynamics:** As women dominate advanced education attainment, organizations must address barriers to retention, promotion, and equitable compensation, especially in industries still grappling with gender imbalances at the executive level.

- **Skills Availability:** A more educated female workforce brings heightened expertise in healthcare, education, psychology, law, and business, but also increasingly in science, technology, engineering, and math (STEM) and data-driven disciplines.

- **Economic Impact:** Education is strongly correlated to earnings and economic mobility, so these trends point to a future where women will have greater financial influence, labor force power, and decision-making authority.

Age

Ageism remains prevalent in the workplace, with 62% of workers aged 50 and older believing that older employees face discrimination and over 93% reporting that it occurs regularly (AARP, 2024). However, this demographic represents an untapped opportunity to enhance workforce stability and facilitate smoother generational transitions. Organizations that neglect to recognize the value of institutional knowledge risk losing a critical asset that, when strategically leveraged, can drive continuity and innovation.

At the same time, age-based bias is not limited to older employees. Younger professionals, particularly those early in their careers or in accelerated leadership paths, are often perceived as inexperienced or unprepared, regardless of their performance or potential. These individuals may face skepticism in high-stakes roles, not due to their capabilities, but rather because of a cultural preference for "paying dues" or a belief that age correlates with wisdom. This perception gap can hinder the development of emerging talent and impede organizational agility. Companies that fail to evaluate talent based on tenure or age, rather than merit and readiness, miss opportunities to develop a dynamic, multigenerational leadership pipeline.

Each generation, whether just entering the workforce or nearing retirement, brings distinct strengths, including digital fluency, fresh ideas, institutional knowledge, and leadership wisdom. However, many organizations fail to create intentional strategies that bridge generational divides, resulting in lost knowledge, underutilized talent, and reduced adaptability.

With millions of roles to fill and seasoned expertise walking out the door, building a multigenerational talent bench is not just a retention strategy; it is a business imperative.

Validity of Traditional Criteria

Beyond assumptions based on personal experience, frames of reference, and individual bias (conscious or unconscious), organizations have also historically relied on non-predictive measures of future performance. In evaluating the potential of the incumbent population, how many leaders will reference or contemplate:

- Years of Education
- Years of Job Experience
- Interest

Extensive research measuring the predictive validity of traditional selection criteria provides incredible insight into poor hiring decisions (Hunter & Hunter, 1998; et al., 2022). The validity estimates for some of the most common assessments are notably weak: years of education ($r = 0.10$), job experience ($r = 0.08$), and interest ($r = 0.26$). Age has an inverse correlation with predicting future performance ($r = -0.01$). These distinct measures do not gain increased predictive validity when combined.

That means many of the factors hiring managers rely on—résumés filled with degrees, long tenure, and assumed interest in a role—have little to no statistical relationship to how someone will perform once hired. It means you can hire someone with all the "right" qualifications on paper and still end up with a disengaged, underperforming employee. It also means that organizations waste millions of dollars annually on selection processes that seem logical but deliver weak results.

In real terms, this translates into costly turnover, misaligned roles, and performance gaps that could have been avoided with more predictive tools. It means the well-liked candidate who "interviews well" but lacks core behavioral traits is likely to underdeliver. It means that high-potential talent may be overlooked because they don't fit a traditional mold—perhaps they are younger, have a non-linear career path, or did not attend a top-tier school. Moreover, it means that companies that don't shift to data-informed, behavior-based hiring are effectively gambling with one of their most important investments: human capital.

The pre-formed and outdated measures of anticipated performance and potential are about as valid as handwriting analysis. **The strongest predictors of talent potential are empirically structured interviews (0.48) and empirically validated strength assessments (0.50).**

Predictive Validity of Assessments

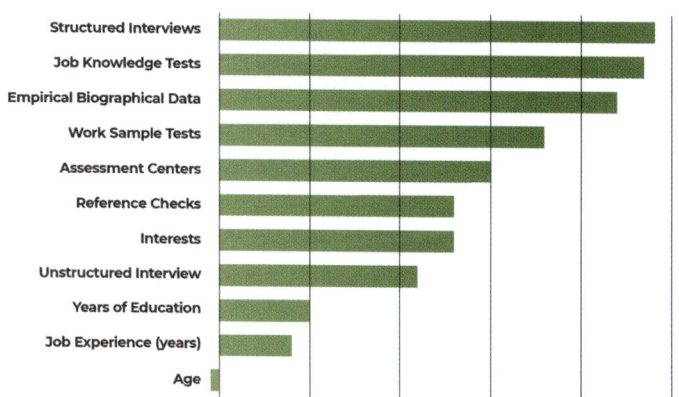

Paul R. Sackett et al., "Revisiting Meta-Analytic Estimates of Validity in Personnel Selection: Addressing Systematic Overcorrection for Restriction of Range," *Journal of Applied Psychology* 107, no. 11 (2022):2040–68, https://doi.org/10.1037/apl0000994.

F.L. Schmidt and J.E. Hunter, "The Validity and Utility of Selection Methods in Personnel Psychology: Practical and Theoretical Implications of 85 Years of Research Findings," *Psychological Bulletin* 124, no. 2 (1998): 262–74.

Validated SELECTION ASSESSMENTS

A structured interview is a systematic and standardized method for assessing candidates. It uses a predetermined set of questions for every individual in the same order and manner. This format minimizes bias and enhances the reliability and validity of the information gathered, as it allows for consistent comparison across respondents.

Structured interviews are grounded in clear objectives and criteria and are aligned with the natural talents validated to predict future success in the role. They promote consistency, improve predictive accuracy in hiring or data collection, and support defensible, evidence-based conclusions by removing variability in how questions are posed and interpreted. Online structured assessments are also viable, provided they offer the same or higher validity.

Several companies provide validated behavior-based assessments (Hogan, Predictive Index, Talent Plus, etc.). When choosing a vendor partner, validity, reliability, cost, quality, efficacy, user-friendliness, customization options, customer support, and cultural alignment should be considered. The following is a high-level summary of the process used to develop a predictive psychometric assessment.

Integrating Validity and Predictive Power
1. Role Analysis and Competency Definition

Purpose: Define the competencies required for success in the role.

- Use psychometric job analysis surveys to quantify the importance, frequency, and complexity of job behaviors.
- Factor analysis may be applied to distill clusters of competencies that statistically align with job success.

2. Development of a Competency-Based Hypothesis

Purpose: Create a testable model predicting which competencies drive job performance.

- Hypothesize which behavioral domains predict performance for the target role (e.g., "Influencing others" predicts sales success).
- May be informed by:
  — Meta-analyses (e.g., Schmidt & Hunter, 1998)
  — Industrial-organizational psychology literature
  — Prior internal validation studies

3. Behavioral Question Design + Predictive Modeling

Purpose: Develop questions designed to tap into the key behavioral predictors of success, and structure them to test criterion-related validity.

- Tag each question to specific competencies and anticipated performance outcomes (e.g., quota attainment, team NPS).
- Field-test questions across a sample population and statistically analyze.
- Techniques used:

- Multiple regression or logistic regression to correlate interview scores with performance ratings or KPIs.
- Item Response Theory (IRT) to assess each question's difficulty and discrimination power.
- Inter-rater reliability analysis (e.g., Cronbach's alpha, ICC)

4. Development of Behavioral Anchored Rating Scales

Purpose: Ensure consistent evaluation of candidate responses.

- Validate anchors through expert panel consensus or Q-sort methodology and test for rater reliability.
- Draw behavior examples for each level from real-world critical incidents that predict high vs. low performance.

5. Structured Interview Pilot and Validation Study

Purpose: Confirm that interview scores predict performance and do not introduce adverse impact.

- Concurrent validation: Interview current employees and compare results to known performance outcomes.
- Predictive validation: Interview new hires using the structure and track outcomes over 6–12 months.
- Correlation analysis (Pearson's r) between interview scores and:
  - Supervisor ratings
  - 90-day success metrics
  - Retention

- — Objective KPIs
- Conduct adverse impact analysis across protected classes (4/5ths rule, z-tests).
- Compare validity coefficients to benchmarks (e.g., .30+ is typically considered moderate predictive validity).

6. Ongoing Refinement and Calibration

Purpose: Maintain effectiveness and fairness of the interview process over time.

- Conduct periodic data audits of interview scores vs. job performance.
- Update questions or scoring guides if predictive validity diminishes.
- Recalibrate raters using scoring simulations and benchmarking.

Summary: Scientific Integrity in Behavioral Interviews

To ensure interviews are more than structured conversations, behavioral science companies add:

- Psychometric validation
- Predictive analytics tied to real-world KPIs
- Ongoing statistical monitoring
- Legal defensibility under EEOC/OFCCP standards
- Calibration for fairness and reliability

This transforms behavioral interviews from artful questioning to data-informed decision tools—grounded in science and designed for high-stakes accuracy.

SAMPLE BEHAVIORAL INTERVIEW VALIDATION MATRIX

Interview Question	Mapped Competency	Performance Metric	Validity Coefficient (r)	Reliability (ICC)	Adverse Impact	Action
"Tell me about a time you had to influence someone resistant to change."	Influence & Persuasion	% Goal Attainment (Sales)	0.42	0.88	None Detected	Keep
"Describe a time when you made a mistake and how you handled it."	Accountability	Supervisor Rating (Integrity)	0.36	0.85	None Detected	Keep
"Give an example of a time you resolved a team conflict."	Team Collaboration	Peer NPS	0.21	0.79	Slight impact (Women < Men)	Revise Anchor Language
"Talk about a time you worked under pressure."	Resilience	90-Day Retention	0.17	0.70	None Detected	Consider Removing
"Tell me about your most creative idea and how you implemented it."	Innovation	Patent Count / Idea Pipeline	0.05	0.68	Significant impact (Race/Ethnicity)	Remove

Explanation of Columns

- **Interview Question:** Actual behavioral question used.

- **Mapped Competency:** The defined behavioral trait being assessed.

- **Performance Metric:** The quantifiable outcome used to test predictive validity (e.g., retention, performance rating, revenue).

- **Validity Coefficient (r):** Correlation between the interview score and performance metric. Typically:
  - 0.10 = small
  - 0.30 = moderate
  - 0.50+ = strong predictive validity

- **Reliability (ICC):** Inter-rater reliability (above 0.75 is considered strong).

- **Adverse Impact:** Notes whether the question produces statistically significant differences across protected groups.

- **Action:** Indicates whether to keep, revise, or remove the question based on all available data.

> **Note:**
> *Validated predictive assessments are the most important human capital investment that delivers the most significant promise of financial return in all future selection and promotional decisions.* **This step is not optional—all other elements of the HCIS hinge on adding science to instinct. The implementation guide, provided after this step, offers insight and direction into identifying and selecting a predictive assessment.**

ACCOUNTING OF HUMAN CAPITAL:
Future Potential

The first task in the AHC was to understand the current HCP's performance and talent composite. Next, assess the future potential of all individuals, excluding those identified as having a planned exit. Examining an individual's strengths using a validated predictive instrument provides a longer-range view of their potential, helping to uncover hidden capabilities or future-fit value.

Employing a validated instrument at this stage enables the leader to verify the original assessment of strong talent within the current role, those on the far right of the AHC matrix. It ensures that investment in further development is directed toward individuals with aligned growth potential.

At the same time, the predictive assessment enables leaders to validate or challenge the assumptions about those with softer talent for the current role, identified as role players, specifically in the upper left quadrant. This helps guard against the impact of unconscious bias that may overshadow a person's contributions or growth capacity.

For individuals who may exhibit softer performance or limited alignment with their current role, it is recommended to include them only if they are a strong cultural contributor and there is a clear intent to reposition them in a role that better aligns with their strengths.

Be prepared, as the AHC Future Potential results may also raise concerns, as many organizations discover their bench strength for growth is not as strong as initially perceived. Future steps will address both the associated risk and the steps to rebalance.

Conclusion

Organizations transition from subjective talent management to evidence-based decision-making by embedding human capital accounting into routine leadership discussions. This begins with employing a clear and comprehensive framework for assessing and evaluating the HCP's health, person by person. A foundation is established by applying predictive rigor and measurement discipline to uncover the powerful intersection of performance, talent, and potential within a workforce.

While this step offers clarity, it also raises essential questions about addressing identified gaps, managing potential exposures, and navigating the complexities of an organization's culture. Assessing human capital is not a simple task. The challenges can provoke hesitation, especially regarding corrective action.

STEP THREE EXPLORES HOW TO STRATIFY AND MANAGE HUMAN CAPITAL RISK BY DIVING INTO THE ORGANIZATION'S RISK TOLERANCE

and the behaviors that must be cultivated to navigate these challenges.

Understanding how to balance risk and opportunity in the HCIS enables leaders to make decisions that protect the dignity of employees and enhance long-term growth and organizational success.

IMPLEMENTING
STEP TWO

I. OVERVIEW & OBJECTIVES

- **Objective**

  Move beyond traditional performance management to a portfolio-based view of human capital. Objectively assess the current talent portfolio using performance, talent, and potential to inform investment decisions.

- **Key Message**

  Talent decisions must be driven by data, not intuition. Just as investors evaluate holdings based on yield, volatility, and growth potential, leaders must evaluate people with equal rigor and intentionality.

II. STEP-BY-STEP ACTION PLAN

1. Gather Comprehensive Performance Data

- **Purpose**

  Create a standardized baseline of individual and team performance across the organization.

- **Actions**

  - Pull data from performance reviews, 360s, KPIs, business results, and team metrics.

- Include contextual metrics such as:
    o Customer satisfaction (NPS)
    o Departmental attrition
    o Engagement scores
    o Time in role
    o Direct reports managed
    o Historical merit increases
- Flag inconsistencies or gaps in performance documentation.

- **Pro Tip**
Performance data should be business aligned and outcome specific—vague ratings degrade decision quality.

2. Assess Talent for the Role

- **Purpose**
Gauge current effectiveness.

- **Actions**

    - Define talent using observable indicators (e.g., adaptability, learning agility, leadership capacity).

    - Separate teachable skills from innate, non-teachable talent.

    - Avoid conflating high performers with high potentials—these are distinct investment profiles.

- **Key Message**
Talent reflects the non-teachable thoughts, feelings, and behaviors that can be developed to near-perfect performance.

3. Assess Potential for the Role

- **Purpose**
Gauge long-term value creation potential, not just current output.

- **Actions**
  - Use validated structured interviews or behavioral assessments.
  - Avoid conflating high performers with high potentials—these are distinct investment profiles.

- **Key Message**
Potential reflects future ROI. Investing in potential is a growth strategy.

4. Mitigate Bias with Third-Party Validation

- **Purpose**
Ensure consistency, fairness, and objectivity in talent assessments.

- **Actions**
  - Facilitate third-party reviews of performance and talent ratings with HR or trained calibrators.
  - Challenge ratings that rely on gut feel,

vague labels (e.g., "fit"), or favoritism.

- Use blind review practices when possible to remove anchoring and bias.

- **Pro Ti**
- If using a person-to-person, custom assessment, conduct periodic inter-rater reliability sessions to drive consistency across evaluators.

5. Visualize the Portfolio

- **Purpose**
Translate performance and talent/potential data into a decision-making tool.

- **Actions**
  - Plot employees on a two-axis talent matrix:
    - o X-axis: Performance
    - o Y-axis: Talent/Potential
  - Segment by department, level, or criticality of role.
  - Identify clusters: those who are performing as *pros*, *high-potentials*, *role players*, and *miscasts* in their current role.

- **Key Message**
You can't optimize what you can't see. Visualization turns data into insight.

III. TOOLS
www.cynthiabentzenmercer.com/resources

- Human Capital Investment Strategy Framework
- Human Capital Attributes Model
- AHC Performance/Talent Matrix
- ACES Talent Tool
- AHC Position Profile Matrix
- Predictive Validity of Assessments Graph

IV. NEXT STEP
With your portfolio visualized and validated, proceed to Step Three: Stratify Risk. This phase shifts focus from assessment to mitigation, identifying where your HCP is most vulnerable and how to safeguard it proactively.

STEP THREE

STRATIFY RISK

Many leaders have a greater fear of knowing than of the unknown.

When we talk about human capital risk, we often think in terms of attrition, succession gaps, or skill shortages. However, there is a more subtle—and equally consequential—risk organizations face when they rely too heavily on familiar patterns: replication bias. One of the most overlooked risks in human capital strategy is the cost of hiring in our own image.

AND NOWHERE IS THIS MORE EVIDENT THAN IN STEM.

CASE STUDY:

Sony Interactive Entertainment Worldwide Studios

The Cost of Homogeneity: A Lesson from the Gaming Industry

In a conversation with Shawn Layden, former Chairman of Sony Interactive Entertainment Worldwide Studios, he recounted the early days of a well-intentioned referral program that rewarded game designers for bringing in talent from their networks. The logic was simple: Smart people know other smart people. But in practice, the result was a homogeneous pipeline, primarily composed of White or Asian male, Stanford-educated coders reflecting their mirror image. It reduced one risk (bad hires) but introduced another: creative stagnation.

This wasn't just a cultural problem; it was a financial one. The executive team began to recognize that game designs were barely evolving. "We kept making new versions of the same game," Layden said. "It was elves in space instead of trolls in space; it was the same product, over and over." The market plateaued. Revenue grew, but only by extracting more value from the same user base, not by expanding it.

That's when the company made an intentional pivotal move. They stopped assuming innovation could come from within the existing design circle and intentionally sought out new voices, particularly women and developers outside of Silicon Valley. The breakthrough came with SingStar, a rhythm game designed and produced by a woman, which opened an entirely new consumer segment. Female gamers became an emerging demographic. What began as an effort to diversify the development team became a masterclass in unlocking market share.

This example isn't just a success story; it's a cautionary tale. Reliance on informal networks, non-predictive assessments, and traditional hiring channels isn't just outdated, it's risky. It limits innovation, reinforces systemic blind spots, and caps future growth.

Strategic risk management in your human capital portfolio means questioning not only who is leaving but also who has never been invited in.

Homogeneity may feel safe, but it is a short-term hedge with long-term liabilities. Risk-adjusted human capital strategies must consider the cost of sameness and the competitive advantage of differences.

The same holds true for organizations. Yet while many understand the importance of diversifying financial portfolios, few apply the same discipline to their most critical asset: human capital. Overreliance on homogeneous talent—whether in terms of background, thought, style, or experience—concentrates risk and constrains growth. Just as a financial advisor would caution against putting all assets into a single stock or sector, organizational leaders must recognize the inherent volatility of a narrowly defined workforce.

Stratifying risk in your HCP means more than demographic representation; it means diversifying skills, perspectives, cognitive approaches, and motivational drivers. It requires examining where your leadership bench is overweighted and where potential is underutilized. It demands hard questions about who gets promoted, who gets heard, and who gets left behind—not just for justice but for performance.

Despite the obvious upside, many leaders fall into the trap of playing small, often driven by fear of the unknown, a lack of confidence, misinformation, or simple ignorance. These limitations prevent them from maximizing their potential returns. Step Three addresses the barriers that hold leaders back—how to confront these challenges, shift the organizational mindset, and overcome cultural norms that may hinder the full realization of human capital investment returns.

After all, the actual value of human capital is not just in identifying risks—it is about lifting the rocks, revealing what lies beneath, and leveraging the HCIS to mitigate those risks effectively. It is a catalyst for innovation, resilience, and competitive advantage.

HUMAN CAPITAL *Risk*

Every organization carries risk in its HCP, but not all risks are visible on the surface. To make strategic investment decisions, leaders must first assess the most immediate exposures within their current workforce. This starts at the incumbent level: Who is currently in the role, how well are they suited to it, and what is their potential for growth? In established organizations, stabilizing and strengthening the existing portfolio is the primary lever for generating returns. Before considering long-term, succession-wide, or structural implications, leaders must first address the current state of roles already occupied.

This section breaks down the five core risk categories within an incumbent portfolio—talent, potential, depth, flight, and diversity—to help organizations conduct a detailed micro-risk assessment. These are the indicators that most directly influence performance, continuity, and future capacity. Evaluating them honestly gives leaders the clarity to act intentionally, protect value, and reallocate investment where it matters most.

TALENT RISK: CURRENT ROLE

When reviewing the output of the AHC matrix, close attention should be paid to the percentage of individuals demonstrating strong talent for their current roles. The target is clear: A minimum of **70%** of your workforce should fall on the right side of the matrix—those who are well matched and aligned with talent for role expectations. This benchmark reflects a healthy portfolio where talent is being effectively deployed.

If the organizational talent is out of balance—if too many incumbents fall into misaligned or underperforming quadrants—this signals an urgent need to recalibrate. Consider adding a specific talent optimization goal to your HCIS Pro Forma. The objective is to raise the percentage of well-matched talent through realignment, development, or role restructuring.

When too few carry too much, overreliance on a small, high-performing group leads to fatigue, burnout, and eventual attrition. Gallup reports that **burned-out employees are 2.6 times more likely to seek a new job**. Moreover, when key talent exits, the pressure only intensifies for those who remain. A well-balanced talent portfolio is not only more productive, but it is also more sustainable. Reviewing AHC results is your first opportunity to spot imbalance and reallocate investment toward strengthening alignment, deepening the bench, and mitigating long-term risk.

WHAT PERCENTAGE OF YOUR HCP HAS TALENT FOR CURRENT ROLES?

POTENTIAL RISK: FUTURE ROLE

A well-balanced HCP must include not only talent aligned to current roles, but individuals with the potential to grow into future leadership. Organizations that actively cultivate internal talent pipelines send a powerful signal to both current employees and prospective candidates: We invest in growth, not just output. This commitment strengthens employee loyalty, enhances retention, and positions the company as a destination for ambitious professionals seeking meaningful career paths, not just job placements.

Yet many organizations fall short in preparing for what's next. When only a handful of individuals are groomed for advancement, the talent bench becomes dangerously thin. This exposes the organization to significant operational, financial, and reputational risk. Critical roles become vulnerable, succession planning falters, and the organization's ability to adapt or scale is severely limited. Overreliance on a select few high performers leads to bottlenecks, burnout, and missed opportunities for innovation and diverse thinking.

In contrast, companies with deep, future-ready talent pipelines are agile and resilient. They can swiftly deploy skilled people to new initiatives, absorb leadership transitions with minimal disruption, and respond to competitive pressures with confidence. However, a lack of structured succession planning remains widespread—only 35% of organizations report having a formal plan for top roles (Deloitte, 2022). This gap creates a cascade of consequences: High-potential employees disengage or leave, institutional knowledge erodes, and the leadership pipeline stalls.

Research consistently shows that internal promotions outperform external hires (Bidwell, 2011). Executives promoted from within fail at nearly half the rate of those hired externally, due to better cultural fit, proven adaptability, and faster ramp-up times. Recognizing this, leading organizations aim for a 2:1 internal-to-external hire ratio—particularly in critical roles—to balance fresh perspective with continuity. While outside talent remains important for injecting new capabilities, overdependence on it often reflects a lack of internal investment and becomes a costly, unsustainable cycle.

Strategic succession planning is more than risk mitigation—it's a long-term talent strategy. It fuels internal mobility, reinforces employer brand equity, and demonstrates a clear commitment to developing people over time. It turns growth into a flywheel: Talent drives business success, which in turn attracts more talent.

Ultimately, a deep, diverse, and resilient talent bench is one of the greatest assets an organization can build. It reduces risk, enhances flexibility, and positions the company to lead in an era defined by constant change. Rebalancing and strengthening the HCP to close these gaps will be the focus of Step Four.

HOW MUCH INTERNAL TALENT POTENTIAL DO YOU HAVE TO DEVELOP FOR GROWTH?

DEPTH RISK

Depth risk occurs when there is either planned attrition, such as retirement, promotion, or coaching out a poor performer, or unplanned attrition, including sudden departures or known flight risks, without a readily available and prepared successor. This risk is particularly acute in executive teams, leader-level roles, and single-incumbent positions where individuals hold deep institutional knowledge, complex stakeholder relationships, or are pivotal to key strategic initiatives.

Best practice suggests that organizations maintain at least three layers of succession depth: a ready-now successor, a candidate who will be ready in 1-2 years, and an emerging talent who may be 3–5 years away. This tiered approach demonstrates the runway and aspiration to grow into the role, mitigating risk and enabling proactive development planning and career pathing.

DEPTH CHART

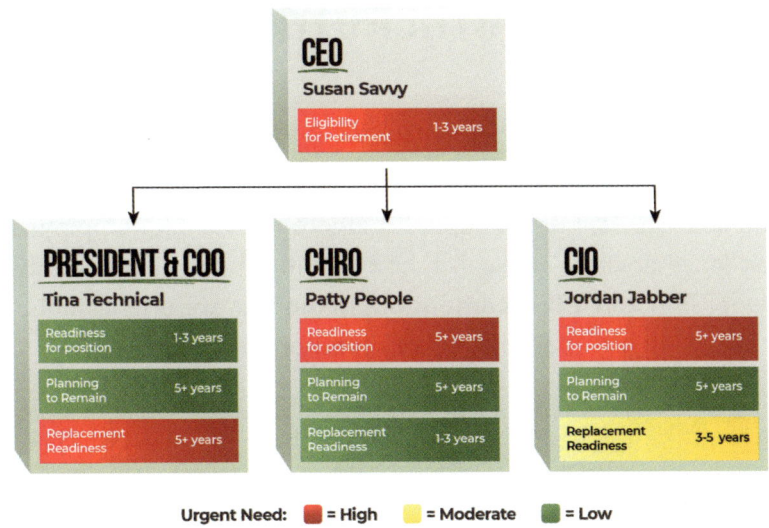

CEO		
Susan Savvy		
Eligibility for Retirement		1-3 years

PRESIDENT & COO		**CHRO**		**CIO**				
Tina Technical		Patty People		Jordan Jabber				
Readiness for position	1-3 years	Readiness for position	5+ years	Readiness for position	5+ years			
Planning to Remain	5+ years	Planning to Remain	5+ years	Planning to Remain	5+ years			
Replacement Readiness	5+ years	Replacement Readiness	1-3 years	Replacement Readiness	3-5 years			

Urgent Need: ■ = High ■ = Moderate ■ = Low

Failure to address depth risk has measurable consequences: a 14% decrease in revenue growth due to leadership voids (McKinsey, 2022), disruption or delay of critical strategic initiatives, loss of competitive advantage, and a 30%–40% slowdown in organizational decision-making following a transition (CCL, 2021–2023). Furthermore, Gartner (2020–2022) highlights that unaddressed depth risk can lead to a breakdown in customer continuity and partner confidence, particularly in externally facing leadership roles. In this context, succession planning is not merely a talent function but a business imperative tied directly to continuity, resilience, and enterprise value.

HOW DEEP IS
YOUR BENCH STRENGTH?

FLIGHT RISK

Flight risk is one of the most significant risks to the HCP. Unlike financial assets, human capital is inherently volatile; employees can leave anytime. Research consistently shows that **effective leadership and advancement opportunities** are crucial factors in retaining high-performing and top-potential employees.

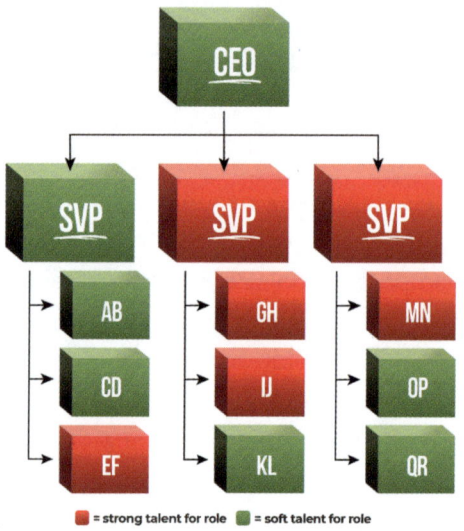

■ = strong talent for role ■ = soft talent for role

Flight Risk

Effective Leadership

Flight risk is most significant when a top-performing or high-potential employee reports to a leader with soft or insufficient talent for their role. This dynamic creates a fundamental misalignment in expectations, support, and developmental opportunity. High-value talent—particularly those who are driven, ambitious, and capable—seek leaders who can challenge them, advocate for their growth, and model strong strategic and people leadership.

When they report to someone who lacks the skills, vision, or presence to lead effectively, it can quickly lead to frustration, disengagement, and a perceived ceiling on their career advancement. These employees often feel underutilized, undervalued, or even stifled, especially if their manager cannot recognize or support their contributions or aspirations. Over time, this mismatch erodes trust and loyalty, making even the most committed individuals more receptive to external opportunities where their potential will be better recognized and nurtured. From a human capital perspective, this is a high-cost loss, not only because of the individual's capability but also because of its potential ripple effect on team morale and organizational momentum.

While serving as the CAO of Mercy, we conducted two studies to quantify the return on investment in talent assessments for nurse leadership roles.

Study One examined the engagement levels of staff reporting to nurse managers with differing degrees of job fit. Nurse leaders identified as having strong talent for the role achieved a 56% excellence rating in engagement, placing them in the 72nd percentile nationally. In contrast, those with only moderate or soft talent for the role received a 39% excellence rating, placing them in the 45th percentile. This 17-point difference in engagement was directly tied to leader capability and alignment with role expectations.

Study Two analyzed team attrition. Nurse leaders with strong talent for their role had an average turnover rate of 18.1%, compared to 21.4% among those with soft talent. That 3.3-point difference equated to approximately 497 fewer nurse departures across the system. Even using a conservative estimate of $20,000 per nurse in replacement costs, the potential savings amounted to nearly $10 million—a powerful demonstration of the financial impact of role alignment and strategic talent investment.

As evidenced, the financial impact of regrettable attrition, the avoidable departure of high-performing or high-potential talent, can be substantial. Research continues to confirm that effective leadership (Gallup, 2019) and advancement opportunities (McKinsey & Company, 2022) are crucial to retaining top talent and high-potential employees. The Work Institute's 2023 Retention Report found that 60% of voluntary turnover is due to poor management.

While the estimates vary widely, the Center for American Progress (CAP) research found that replacing a highly skilled employee costs about 200% of their annual salary. Furthermore, according to SHRM, **the direct and indirect costs of replacing key talent, including recruitment, onboarding, and lost productivity, can exceed 50% of annual profits in specific industries.**

The long-term impact is slower revenue growth and lower customer satisfaction (Boston Consulting Group, 2024). Beyond the financial toll, losing top talent also has long-term effects on revenue growth, customer satisfaction, company morale, and overall brand reputation.

HOW VOLATILE IS YOUR HCP?

ATTRITION DISRUPTION RISK EVALUATION

With the various individual risk categories in mind (talent, potential, depth, flight), a Talent Risk Evaluation Matrix can provide a comprehensive overview of volatility, aggregating multiple risk dimensions into a single, actionable score to understand the risk of avoidable attrition. The analytical rigor quantifies the risk exposure tied to specific roles or individuals across the organization.

It does not just flag turnover risk—it offers a strategic view of where talent vulnerabilities intersect with business criticality. Leaders can finally move from anecdote to algorithm when deciding where to focus succession planning, knowledge transfer, or targeted retention efforts.

Each role or individual is assessed across five weighted factors:

- **Retention Risk:** How likely is departure, either voluntary or involuntary?

- **Strategic Criticality:** How essential is this talent to enterprise priorities?

- **Replacement Difficulty:** How hard is finding or ramping up a viable successor?

- **Performance Volatility:** How consistently does this individual perform in a changing environment?

- **Knowledge Loss Risk:** Would departure result in losing legacy, proprietary, or undocumented expertise?

Example Formula:

Talent Risk Index = (Retention Risk x 0.3) + (Strategic Criticality x 0.25) + (Replacement Difficulty x 0.2) + (Performance Volatility x 0.15) + (Knowledge Loss Risk x 0.1)

Category	Score (0–10)	Weight	Weighted Score
Retention Risk	6	0.3	1.8
Strategic Criticality	8	0.25	2
Replacement Difficulty	7	0.2	1.4
Performance Volatility	5	0.15	0.75
Knowledge Loss Risk	4	0.1	0.4
Total			6.35

The result is a composite score, often visualized in a color-coded ddashboard:

- **Low Risk (0–3):** Stable roles with low business disruption potential

- **Medium Risk (4–6):** Moderate exposure requiring monitoring or mitigation

- **High Risk (7–10):** Urgent action needed to reduce vulnerability

NAME	TITLE	x 0.3 RETENTION RISK	x 0.25 PERFORMANCE VOLATILITY	x 0.2 STRATEGIC CRITICALITY	x 0.15 REPLACEMENT DIFFICULTY	x 0.1 KNOWLEDGE LOSS RISK	RISK SCORE
Tabitha Able	Chief Marketing Officer	Low = 1	Low = 1	Low = 1	Low = 1	Low = 1	1
John Joe	Chief Financial Officer	High = 10	High = 10	High = 10	High = 10	High = 10	10
Susie Que	Chief People Officer	High = 10	Low = 1	High = 10	High = 5	High = 1	6
Tracy Smith	Chief Operations Officer	Med. = 5	Med. = 5	Med. = 5	Med. = 5	Med. = 5	5

This diagnostic tool transforms subjective conversations about "who might leave" into data-driven insights about where your human capital is most at risk—and where strategic investment is required to protect enterprise value.

DIVERSIFICATION RISK

In human capital strategy, as in finance, diversification is essential to optimizing performance while minimizing risk. Homogeneity—whether in background, experience, or perspective—can create a false sense of alignment but ultimately leads to stagnation, group-think, and greater exposure to disruption. In today's competitive market, where talent shortages persist (see Step One), diversification is not just a social imperative; it is a business necessity.

When evaluating the composition of an organization's HCP, consistent patterns of underrepresentation, especially when paired with widespread assessments labeling individuals as "soft talent," should raise immediate red flags. If women, people of color, older workers, or other historically underrepresented groups are systematically rated as lacking natural talent, the issue may not be with the talent itself, but with the tools and biases embedded in the evaluation process. Poorly designed or non-validated assessments not only risk adverse impact claims but also undermine the organization's ability to identify and develop its true high-potential talent.

A growing body of research highlights the **subjectivity** embedded in talent identification and performance management. Studies show that **women and employees from racially diverse backgrounds often receive more ambiguous, personality-focused feedback.** At the same time, White male counterparts are more likely to receive actionable, skill-based feedback that directly connects to business outcomes (Correll & Simard, 2016). For example, women are often described as lacking leadership presence or lacking confidence. In contrast, men in similar situations are advised to demonstrate strategic thinking, a subtle yet critical distinction that significantly influences how they are perceived in leadership evaluations. Likewise, Black and Latino employees are often evaluated on interpersonal skills rather than their direct contributions to business outcomes, a trend that can hinder advancement opportunities.

Additionally, age bias in performance evaluation disproportionately affects employees over 50, particularly in industries that favor digital fluency and innovation. Research by the National Bureau of Economic Research (2020) suggests that **older employees are often assumed to be less adaptable, even when their performance metrics match or exceed those of younger colleagues.** If talent reviews systematically assign lower potential scores to older employees based on assumptions rather than evidence, organizations risk losing seasoned professionals who bring deep institutional knowledge and mentorship capabilities.

The impact of these biases extends beyond individual careers—it shapes an organization's leadership pipeline, innovation capacity, and long-term strategic strength. When performance and talent evaluation methods disproportionately categorize certain groups as soft talent for the role, it limits the pool of individuals considered for advancement and stifles diversity at the top. This, in turn, creates a self-reinforcing cycle where leadership remains homogeneous, reinforcing outdated norms about who belongs in high-impact roles.

Before proceeding further with HCIS steps, organizations must ensure that their talent evaluation processes are equitable, transparent, and aligned with business objectives. Failing to do so risks reinforcing systemic biases, limiting access to opportunity, and ultimately undermining the effectiveness of an HCIS. By recognizing and correcting these disparities, companies can build a more resilient, diverse, and high-performing workforce that reflects the best talent. Step Four will cover the path to performance- and potential-based portfolio balancing, aiming to increase diversification and mitigate risk.

HOW DIVERSIFIED IS YOUR EXISTING HCP? HOW CONFIDENT ARE YOU IN YOUR ORGANIZATION'S ASSESSMENT TOOLS?

ORGANIZATIONAL *Risk*

An organization's risk tolerance around human capital reveals the underlying culture that shapes how people are valued, developed, and empowered. Organizations poised to unlock the force multiplier potential of a well-executed HCIS operate from a belief that talent is not just a resource, but a renewable strategic advantage. They actively reframe human capital from a labor cost to an asset worthy of investment, stewardship, and accountability.

Culturally, these organizations foster a psychological safety environment where data-informed talent assessments are viewed as tools for growth and alignment, rather than a threat. They are willing to invest the time and energy to conduct a comprehensive accounting of talent, grounded in transparency and trust. These cultures also demonstrate the courage to look at performance and potential objectively, embracing the predictive, even when it challenges the familiar. There is a genuine curiosity to explore how diversity in background, thought, and approach can create a more agile and resilient organization, and a shared commitment to act on those insights.

Most importantly, the culture supportsbroad-based leadership accountability, where every leader is expected to understand, model, and reinforce the HCIS, ensuring it is not a siloed HR initiative but an integral part of how the organization operates. In these environments, talent stewardship is not confined to the C-suite—it is part of the leadership DNA at every level. This kind of culture does not just tolerate the risks associated with a strategic human capital approach—it is energized by them, knowing that meaningful transformation only happens when the organization is brave and aligned enough to see people as the actual engine of enterprise value.

CULTURAL RISK TOLERANCE

While much of this strategy relies on analytics, forecasts, and investment principles, its success is ultimately determined by something less tangible but far more influential: organizational culture.

For some organizations, the insights revealed through HCIS implementation will evoke discomfort. Not because the methodology is unclear—on the contrary, the framework is grounded in data and designed to be practical and measurable. The discomfort stems from what the data may challenge: **longstanding cultural norms, unwritten rules, and leadership behaviors that have gone unexamined or unchallenged for too long.**

Some cultures pride themselves on speed and consensus, often at the expense of quality and candor. Others value stability so deeply that they default to legacy practices over fresh, evidence-based insight. In many organizations, performance conversations are muted by a desire to preserve harmony, avoid hard decisions, or protect long-tenured employees from disruption. Although often well-intentioned, these cultural reflexes create blind spots that directly hinder the HCIS's strategic potential.

Implewell intentioned requires a performance- and potential-focused mindset at the cultural level—not just in HR or the executive suite, but embedded across every talent-related decision. It demands that the organization trade intuition for insight, tradition for truth, and habit for evidence. It calls for replacing outdated notions of "fairness" (where everyone is treated the same) with a more sophisticated form of equity that aligns investment with impact and reward with results.

Nevertheless, make no mistake: this kind of cultural shift comes with risk. Not all organizations are ready to see what the data reveals. Some will resist, clinging to anecdotal wisdom, subjective evaluations, or vague notioTs of "fit." Others will question whether quantifying human potential is too impersonal, too transactional. Still others will default to "either/or" thinking—believing one must choose between performance and diversity, between rigor and compassion, between truth and loyalty.

These cultural risks are predictable and addressable but ignoring them will stall progress before it begins. Culture is the gatekeeper of any strategic transformation. Suppose the culture lacks the tolerance for honest assessment. In that case, the diaddressable,investment-based thinking, or the appetite for rebalancing talent portfolios, will cause even the most elegant HCIS playbook to sit unused.

This is why the heavy lifting must extend beyond incumbent analysis. Once performance and potential are clarified at the individual level, the more complex—and often more consequential—work begins, confronting systemic cultural norms. How we hire, how we reward, how we confront underperformance, and how we elevate are all shaped by the values we protect and the decisions we're willing to make.

Organizations that outperform the market do not get there by accident. They deliberately create cultures that value truth over tradition, evidence over ego, and courage over comfort. If you lead with performance and potential, the rest—diversity, engagement, innovation—will follow.

Is your culture ready to know the truth?

AND MORE IMPORTANTLY, READY TO ACT ON IT?

Cultural Red Flags That Undermine HCIS Success

Even the most rigorous HCIS can be derailed by a culture that resists evidence, avoids conflict, or prioritizes comfort over clarity. Watch for these cultural red flags—they are often early indicators that your organization may not be ready to yield strategic returns from its HCP.

Speed Over Rigor

A "move fast" mentality that celebrates urgency over accuracy often leads to shortcuts in selection, development, and promotion decisions, undermining long-term value in favor of short-term optics.

Niceness Over Candor

Cultures that prize harmony over truth discourage the honest conversations necessary to assess performance, confront underperformance, and identify high-potential talent. Avoiding discomfort compromises credibility and stalls growth.

Legacy Loyalty Over Data

When decisions are based on tenure, familiarity, or tradition—rather than capability and potential—organizations reward stagnation and reinforce outdated power structures.

Subjectivity Over Structure
A resistance to structured assessments, validated tools, or predictive analytics in favor of "gut feel" or "manager discretion" introduces bias, inconsistency, and missed opportunity.

Uniformity Over Differentiation
Cultures that believe fairness means treating everyone the same fail to invest where it matters most. HCIS requires differentiated investment that is aligned with contribution, potential, and return.

Fear of Transparency
If there's discomfort around sharing performance data, succession depth, or internal mobility gaps, the culture may be protecting status quo at the expense of strategy.

Overreliance on External Hires
Organizations that consistently default to external hires, especially for leadership roles, may signal a lack of confidence in internal development and a weak succession pipeline.

If you cannot talk honestly about performance, you cannot invest in it. HCIS success depends on metrics and the courage and cultural readiness to act on what the metrics reveal. Use the following questions to surface cultural enablers and inhibitors.

Not at All (1) Somewhat (2) Absolutely (3)
1. Are leaders empowered to speak candidly about underperformance without fear of political fallout?

2. Do we have a culture that values data over anecdote?

3. When confronted with hard truths from data, do we act?

4. Do we routinely challenge assumptions about what makes someone "high potential" or "a good fit"?

5. Are we willing to stop doing familiar things that are no longer effective?

A score of 13-15 represents a strong cultural appetite. Scores of 5 – 8 would suggest that significant cultural preparedness will be necessary to overcome the inherent risk to the organization. Those that fall in the middle are most common and ripe for evolution. Part Two: Enabling an Investment Culture will address organizational readiness at a deeper level.

LEADER RISK TOLERANCE

The most significant place where organizational readiness presents itself is in leader behavior. The pace and trajectory of success in human capital investment are ultimately determined by the CEO and leadership team's confidence and competence in executing the HCIS. This is not just a matter of implementing best practices—it requires a leadership mindset that balances analytical rigor, strategic foresight, and the courage to act decisively.

Organizations that excel in human capital investment are led by executives who understand the science of talent, recognize the financial impact of human capital decisions, and are confident to make bold, informed moves. However, this balance of confidence and competence is not always present, and when either element is missing, the organization's ability to maximize its workforce potential is significantly compromised. Just as an investor's risk tolerance dictates how they approach financial strategy, so does leader risk tolerance impact HCIS.

Leader Risk Personas

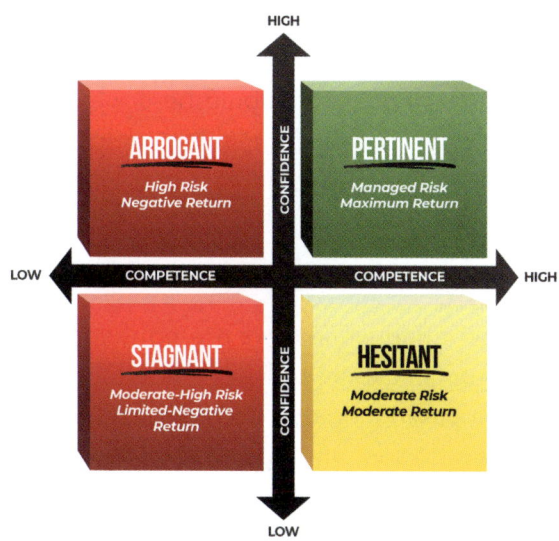

Stagnant:
The leader hesitates to take risks, is overly reliant on out-dated talent models, and is slow to respond to shifting workforce dynamics. Their uncertainty results in missed opportunities, ineffective teams, and an overall lack of agility, posing a moderate-to-high risk for the organization. Stagnant leaders rely on the status quo.

Arrogant:
The leader dismisses research, ignores predictive analytics, and makes critical human capital decisions based on gut instinct or outdated traditions. This is the most dangerous scenario, as overconfidence and incompetence can lead to devastating miscalculations, eroding the organization's ability to attract, retain, and develop high-performing talent. This leader thinks they know best.

Hesitant:
The leader's hesitation—often due to fear of resistance

from senior leadership, discomfort with challenging ingrained norms, or concerns about disrupting organizational culture—causes them to move too cautiously. They understand what should be done but hesitate to take the necessary steps, resulting in lost opportunities for competitive advantage. Hesitant leaders value people-pleasing over risk-taking.

Pertinent:

The most effective leaders are confident and competent in human capital strategy execution. They embrace evidence-based methods, commit to transparent performance evaluation, and make talent decisions that drive long-term organizational success. These leaders position their companies to cultivate potential by strategically investing in their workforce, ensuring that human capital is managed and optimized as a financial asset.

The most significant opportunity for transformation lies in developing the confidence of leaders who possess the necessary knowledge but struggle to take action. These leaders often hesitate to make the bold decisions necessary to elevate organizational performance, whether due to personal relationships, a desire for approval, or the fear of disrupting established processes. Unlocking their potential requires a structured approach to change management that helps leaders navigate resistance, build trust, and execute human capital strategies with conviction.

TAKE A MOMENT TO CONSIDER THE TOP TWO TO THREE LAYERS OF LEADERSHIP.

Part Two: Enabling an Investment Culture will explore how organizations can bridge the gap between competence and confidence, equipping leaders with the tools and frameworks to make talent decisions that yield sustainable, market-leading results.

RISK ASSESSMENT

Understanding the organizational risk before embarking on Steps Four to Six is crucial. The risk assessment requires data derived from Steps Two and Three and the rater's qualitative organizational readiness assessment. The HCIS risk assessment template can be downloaded at **www.cynthiabentzenmercer.com/resources.**

It is important to note that the rating definitions and scales are illustrative. Understanding the industry, location, positions, and best-in-class benchmarks is crucial for calibrating the assessment. Additionally, weighting ratings to emphasize areas that require more focus may benefit the company's priorities. Organizations gain a strategic advantage in talent retention and succession planning by treating human capital risks as business-critical factors.

HCIS RISK ASSESSMENT

HCIS Risk Assessment	HIGH RISK (3)	MED. RISK (2)	LOW RISK (1)	RATING	ILLUSTRATIVE EXAMPLES & RANGES | SHOULD BE BASED ON INDUSTRY, LOCATION, AND BEST-IN-CLASS BENCHMARKS
Human Capital Risk					
Current Talent for Role	<50%	50 - 70%	>70%	3	Percentage of employees with strong talent for current role
Future Talent Potential	<30%	30 - 50%	>50%	3	Percentage of employees with strong talent for next level role based on predicitive assessment
Depth Risk (key positions)	0	1 - 2	3	2	Number of named successors for each key role
Flight / Attrition Disprution Risk	>20%	10 - 20%	<10%	1	Percentage of flight risk or attrition disruption risk among a critical group or position
Diversification Risk					
Gender	<20%	<30%	>40%	2	Percentage of women, particularly in leadership roles
Age	2 gen	3 gen	4 gen	1	Number of generations actively participating in the workforce
Race/Ethnicity	homogeneous	moderate diversity	heterogeneous	3	Degree of diversity, particularly in leadership roles
Organizational Readiness					
Company Risk Tolerance	5 - 8	9 - 12	13 - 15	3	
Leader Risk Tolerance	<50%	50 - 80%	>80%	2	Percentage of leaders in positions of influence that are Pertinent (highly competent and confident)
			RISK SCORE	2.2	

Conclusion

Risk is an inherent part of any investment strategy, and human capital is no exception. Understanding, assessing, and stratifying risk separates reactive organizations from those that lead the market. By evaluating talent, potential, depth, flight, diversification, and organizational risks, leaders gain the clarity to anticipate challenges rather than merely respond to them.

The most effective organizations do not view risk as something to be feared but as a factor to be strategically managed. Leaders who understand their own risk tolerance and their organization's broader cultural risk tolerance can make more informed, data-driven decisions that strike a balance between stability and opportunity. They avoid reckless overconfidence and excessive caution, instead making measured, high-return investments in talent.

With a clear understanding of human capital risk, leaders are now equipped to take the next critical step: rebalancing talent investments to achieve optimal returns. Step Four will focus on adjusting and reallocating human capital to maximize strategic advantage, ensuring the right talent is in the right place at the right time. Organizations can continuously refine their portfolios by treating talent as a financial asset, unlocking more significant innovation, resilience, and long-term value

IMPLEMENTING
STEP THREE

I. OVERVIEW & OBJECTIVES

- **Objective**
  Identify and quantify risk within the HCP. Move from reactive talent management to proactive risk mitigation by exposing vulnerabilities across leadership, succession, performance, and diversity dimensions.

- **Key Message**
  Talent concentration, succession gaps, and cultural blind spots are as dangerous to business continuity as financial overexposure. Smart investors hedge their bets. Smart leaders do the same with people.

II. STEP-BY-STEP ACTION PLAN

1. Identify Immediate Human Capital Risks

- **Purpose**
  Conduct a risk audit of your current workforce based on performance, potential, role criticality, and volatility.

- **Actions**
  - Review Accounting of Human Capital matrix to pinpoint:

- o Underperformers in high-impact roles
- o Critical roles lacking succession plans
- o *High potentials* nearing disengagement
— Partner with HR to flag known risk indicators (e.g., exit interviews, absenteeism, manager instability).
— Talent Risk Scorecard (performance x potential x role criticality)

- **Pro Tip**
  Start with your top 20% of value-driving roles—what happens if one key player exits unexpectedly?

2. Evaluate Specific Risk Dimensions

- **Talent & Potential Risk**
  — Actions
    - o Assess whether rising talent is being underleveraged or overexposed.
    - o Examine robustness of leadership pipeline across business units.
  — Key Message
    Overreliance on *pros* and *high potentials* increases fragility.

- **Flight Risk**
  — Definition
    Risk of losing high performers or *high potentials* due to disengagement or outside offers.

- Indicators
  - o Stalled promotions
  - o Below-benchmark pay
  - o Weak manager relationships
  - o Lack of career clarity
- **Depth Risk**
  - Definition
    Insufficient layers of succession readiness.
  - Best Practice
    Maintain "ready now," "ready in 1–2 years," and "emerging 3–5 years" for all critical roles.
- **Diversification Risk**
  - Definition
    Overconcentration of homogenous thinking or demographic representation in leadership.
  - Actions
    - o Analyze leadership demographics.
    - o Audit interview and promotion bias.
    - o Ensure assessments do not have adverse impact.
- **Organizational Risk**
  - Leader risk tolerance (risk aversion vs overconfidence)
  - Cultural readiness for transparency and talent investment

- **Key Message**
Strategy without cultural risk tolerance leads to stagnation.

3. Conduct a Comprehensive Risk Assessment

- **Purpose**
Quantify portfolio-wide human capital risk to prioritize interventions and mitigation strategies.
- **Actions**
  — Use HCIS risk rating criteria:
    o Talent for role
    o Talent potential
    o Flight risk
    o Depth of succession
    o Diversity contribution
    o Cultural and leadership risk readiness
  — Assign weighted scores to each factor and generate risk heat maps.
- **Pro Tip**
Map results against business continuity plans to determine exposure by function, geography, or customer segment.

4. Develop Targeted Mitigation Plans

- **Purpose**
Move from insight to action by creating tailored

responses to talent risk.

- **Actions**
  - For **high flight risk employees:** Initiate stay conversations and offer development or visibility opportunities.
  - For **succession gaps:** Accelerate development for internal successors or start external pipeline building.
  - For **diversity risks:** Ensure underrepresented talent is visible in promotion paths and development programs.
  - For **cultural risks:** Train managers and leadership teams in strategic courage and data-based decision-making.
- **Key Message**
  You do not eliminate risk—you manage and price it into your leadership model.

5. Establish Risk Monitoring Protocols

- **Purpose**
  Track human capital risk dynamically—just like operational or financial risk.
- **Actions**
  - Create quarterly talent risk dashboards for executive review.
  - Track:
    - o Leadership succession coverage
    - o Engagement of pros

o   Emerging turnover signals

o   Bench strength for critical roles

- **Pro Tip**
  Overlay business strategy timelines with people risk maps to identify potential derailers before they occur.

6. Link Risk to Investment Decisions

- **Purpose**
  Translate risk data into actionable human capital investment plans.

- **Actions**

  — Redirect resources toward risk-prone talent segments.

  — Use risk scores to inform performance improvement, retention efforts, and mobility planning.

  — Tie risk mitigation efforts directly to future workforce forecasting.

- **Key Message**
  Where the portfolio is weakest is where the investment case is strongest—if you act early.

III. TOOLS

www.cynthiabentzenmercer.com/resources

- Human Capital Investment Strategy Framework
- Depth Chart

- Flight Risk Chart
- Attrition Disruption Risk Evaluation
- Leader Risk Personas
- HCIS Risk Assessment

IV. NEXT STEP
- **Forward Path**

  With human capital risk identified and mitigation plans in motion, move to Step Four: Rebalance Allocations. This next step is about redistributing resources, support, and development where they'll generate the highest return and reduce portfolio volatility.

STEP FOUR

REBALANCE
ALLOCATIONS

**Intestinal fortitude increases when
you add science to your gut.**

Sarah was a force of nature. While her peers were closing deals steadily, she was outselling them five to one. Then ten to one. Soon, she was not only the top salesperson in the company but was also breaking historic records for the entire brand. Clients loved her, her numbers were unmatched, and she was single-handedly driving revenue growth. However, there was a problem.

Sarah was terrible at paperwork. Expense reports piled up, and administrative deadlines were missed. Her manager, growing frustrated, felt she was setting a bad example, and the situation escalated.

Despite her record-breaking sales, discussions about

terminating her employment began. After all, fairness means holding everyone to the same standard, right? That was when the HR leader stepped in and suggested that, rather than firing her, they assign her an assistant. The boss balked, concerned that it was not fair to the others. The HR leader suggested that when others sell at her level, they can also have an assistant. Reluctantly, the boss agreed.

Fairness often means treating everyone the same—offering equal access, applying uniform standards, and distributing resources evenly. But justice goes a step further. Justice recognizes that not everyone starts from the same place or has faced the same barriers, and therefore requires intentionally different actions to ensure equitable outcomes. Justice asks: What adjustments must we make to remove systemic friction? It's not about lowering standards—it's about elevating opportunity and removing blind spots that prevent human capital from being fully seen, supported, and cultivated.

One year later, Sarah outperformed her peers ten to one and then twenty to one. With administrative burdens off her plate, she could focus entirely on what she did best: selling.

Fairness may have cost the company its most valuable asset. Justice acknowledged that different people bring unique strengths—and that sometimes, achieving success requires providing individuals with what they need to thrive. Just as one would not arbitrarily invest the same percentage into each asset type or even sector within a fund class, we must allocate our resources strategically and intentionally.

....

ASSET-BASED *Investment*

While the financial value of human capital is well documented, traditional approaches to talent management often fail to consider the psychological factors that drive performance. Employees are not simply units of production but individuals with unique strengths, motivations, and potential.

Organizations have approached talent development through a deficit-based model for decades—identifying weaknesses, diagnosing performance gaps, and developing corrective measures to "fix" employees. Performance reviews often focus on areas for improvement rather than amplify areas of excellence. Leadership development programs aim to address perceived deficiencies rather than sharpen innate strengths. The implicit assumption in much of corporate talent strategy has been that employees are malleable—blank slates who can be shaped into top performers in any role with enough training, coaching, and feedback. At this point, we have dispelled that myth.

In a rapidly changing business environment, where agility and engagement are crucial,

ORGANIZATIONS THAT FULLY LEVERAGE THE POTENTIAL OF THEIR PEOPLE GAIN A SIGNIFICANT STRATEGIC ADVANTAGE.

They develop deep talent pipelines that are aligned with their vision. They attract and retain high performers who feel valued and energized by their work. They create cultures where excellence is the norm, not because employees are forced to improve their weaknesses but because they are empowered to maximize their strengths.

By understanding the science of strengths, redefining how we evaluate potential, and shifting from a deficit-based to an asset-based approach to leadership, organizations can unlock extraordinary performance levels for their people and their bottom line.

....

RISK-ADJUSTED *Return*

In investment, a risk-adjusted return measures an asset's potential reward relative to its risk or volatility level. High-growth stocks present considerable upside but necessitate careful monitoring and investment. The same principle applies to human capital: top talent offers exponential value but requires intentional cultivation.

Many organizations adopt a maintenance approach to talent, fixing problems rather than fostering growth. This is similar to retaining underperforming assets, hoping they will recover. Instead, leaders should concentrate on high-growth employees, ensuring they have the resources, opportunities, and motivation to deliver long-term value.

When weighing risk versus return, it is essential to reconsider the difference between human capital's teachable and non-teachable components. **The most significant risk to HCIS is a limited talent pool.** As discussed in Step Two, knowledge and skills can be taught, and with proper investment in training, these gaps can be closed relatively swiftly. **On the other hand, natural talent must already be present to be developed to near-perfect performance.**

According to Buckingham and Clifton (2001), most organizations are built on two flawed assumptions: that everyone can learn to be competent in almost anything, and that everyone's most significant room for growth lies in their areas of greatest weakness. In line with positive psychology, the authors argue that instead, each employee's talents require continual development, and **every person's most significant room for growth lies in areas of their greatest strength.**

Selecting and promoting individuals with strong talent for a role, while providing education to close skill and knowledge gaps, yields the greatest return on investment. Developing talent to its full potential produces a competitive advantage. The opposite is also true.

When leaders are determined to improve an area of lesser talent, time and investment are wasted. While the individual may marginally improve in a non-teachable area, there is little upside value. This is one of the organization's most significant miscalculations, resulting in diminishing returns. Having conviction in this concept is vital to the effectiveness of the rebalancing plan.

··

Rebalancing PLAN

It is essential to remember that everyone possesses talent and potential; the question is, for what? As such, everyone can be a pro when in the *right role*, on the *right team*, and in the *right company*. Read that carefully. This is not a contradiction to strength development. It does not mean everyone can be trained to be great at anything. It does, however, mean that the AHC is not an assignment of labels. It assesses performance in, and talent for, a *particular role*.

It is up to the individual to determine where they choose to share their human capital, and it is the organization's fiscal responsibility to rebalance when there is a misalignment.

AHC Rebalancing Path Forward

Using the data from the AHC, each quadrant requires a specific rebalancing path forward: recast/exit, monitor, invest, or optimize. Just as you do not ignore underperforming funds or those that perform only modestly, misallocated human capital must also be addressed at the individual position level.

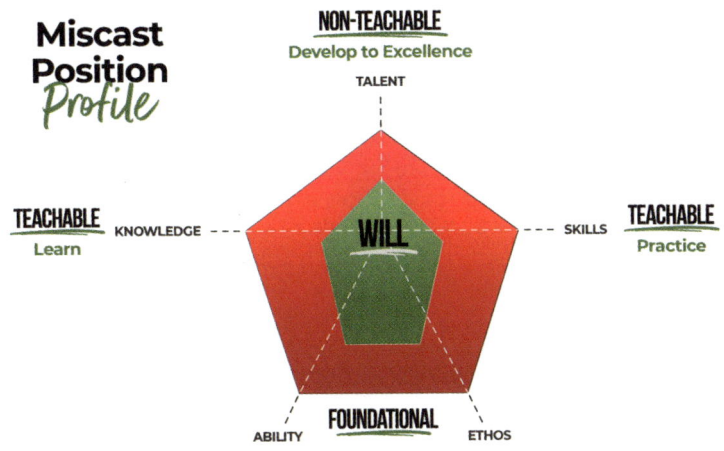

Source: Copyright 2023, Talent Plus®, Lincoln, Nebraska.

Every investor periodically evaluates assets to determine whether to hold, sell, or reposition them. The same applies to teams. Research from Gallup shows that employees with low natural talent for a role require three times more development effort to achieve competency, yet they often never outperform a naturally suited counterpart. Rather than forcing a poor match, one of the most immediate actions is to implement a plan to address those who are not performing and lack the requisite talent for the position. Remembering that everyone has talent, it is recommended to consider whether the individual could be better suited for a job that aligns with their talent, provided that they are well aligned with the company's ethos.

When recasting is not an option, it is important to follow the corrective action guidelines outlined by the human resources department to ensure that no other extenuating circumstances have impacted their performance. If performance improvement plans are unsuccessful, the most dignified course of action is to separate, allowing the person to find a position that aligns with their natural talents.

Failing to exit or recast a poor performer has numerous financial repercussions:

- **Output:** Underperformers can create a bottleneck, often slowing down the productivity of others. This can cause incredible frustration on the part of the incumbent pros.

- **Culture:** As noted in Step Two, company culture is shaped and nurtured by the individuals you select, develop, and promote. When underperformers are allowed to remain on teams, a culture of mediocrity spreads.

- **Time:** Leaders spend more time with underperformers, reducing the time to invest in high-potential individuals.

- **Regrettable Attrition:** Strong performers want to work on winning teams. They leave when forced to work alongside those who do not put forth the same quality and effort.

- **Customer Experience:** When employees struggle to perform, it impacts everyone around them, including the customer.

Investors would not allow a failing fund to remain in their financial portfolio indefinitely. **Identifying performance challenges and addressing them swiftly is the most fiscally responsible action.**

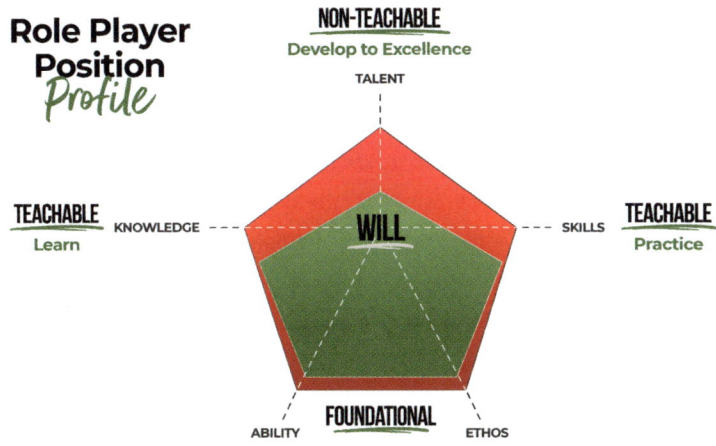

Role Player Position *Profile*

NON-TEACHABLE
Develop to Excellence
TALENT

TEACHABLE
Learn
KNOWLEDGE

WILL

SKILLS
TEACHABLE
Practice

FOUNDATIONAL
ABILITY · ETHOS

There are times when a fund is placed on a watch list when considering the financial portfolio. Perhaps the returns are positive, but the investment's ongoing success depends on other variables. The same is true for individuals who meet performance expectations but do not demonstrate the requisite non-teachable talent for the role.

To illustrate this concept with an overt example, consider the individual who possesses in-depth institutional knowledge and is responsible for a highly technical role. Perhaps the employee executes the work precisely, but they often exhibit rude behavior towards their colleagues or display a negative attitude. Leaders often retain these employees for fear of losing their expertise, overlooking the implications of their behavior. It is essential to consider whether individuals with strong performance but limited talent for the role contribute more than they withdraw.

In other situations, softer talent for the role can be mitigated by partnering the individual with others. Though the individual's utility is more limited, they may serve as a strong role player. However, it is essential to recognize that performance may be contingent upon the leader, the team, or the job design. A leader may help soften their edges, a team member may complement an area of softer talent, or the job description could be crafted to minimize the focus on the lesser area of talent.

Role players can be an intentional component of the HCP. However, these individuals should be regularly monitored to ensure performance remains at its peak, especially if there is a change in leadership or team dynamics. Alternatively, if the person is hindering progress and blocking the path of an individual with high potential, they should be exited or recast.

Strong discernment must be given to the top left quadrant of the HCP. **It is natural for leaders to want to retain those with long tenure and deep institutional knowledge. However, they often minimize the enhanced level of performance that is possible with complementary talent for the role.** This will be quantified later in this step.

INVEST: HIGH POTENTIALS

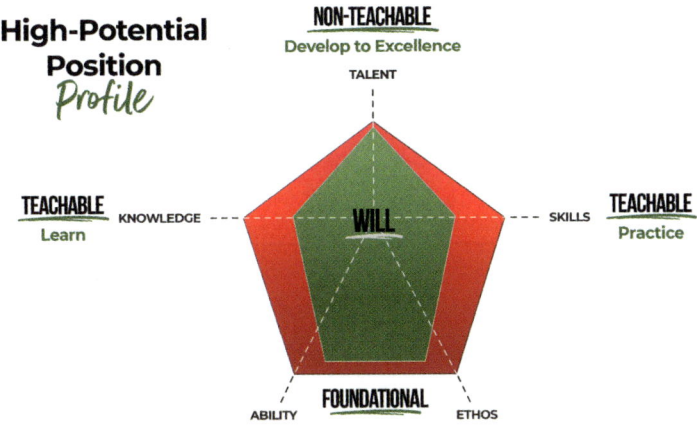

In finance, investors prioritize assets with the highest growth potential. Similarly, leaders should aggressively invest in top talent. These individuals drive innovation, culture, and long-term success.

While these individuals have strong talent for their roles, they are not yet performing to the top of their abilities. This is usually based on time spent in the position. Individuals new to a company or job may require time to develop the knowledge and skills necessary for peak performance.

It is essential to understand the cause of performance limitations (i.e., will or skill) and actively work to coach them to their full potential.

- *Are the role expectations clear?*
- *Has there been ample training?*
- *Does the individual have the requisite ability?*
- *Are there resource limitations, such as software, hardware, or staff?*

Having a career investment discussion with a high-potential

employee is vital. **Individuals with strong talent for the role want to excel and strive for success.** Working with them on an accelerated growth plan can provide the guidance and direction to advance their development.

This is the farm team. A deep investment in developing talent and teaching knowledge and skills promises the greatest return on investment. However, if the individual continues to underperform over time, a reassessment of alignment for the role should be explored.

OPTIMIZE: PROS

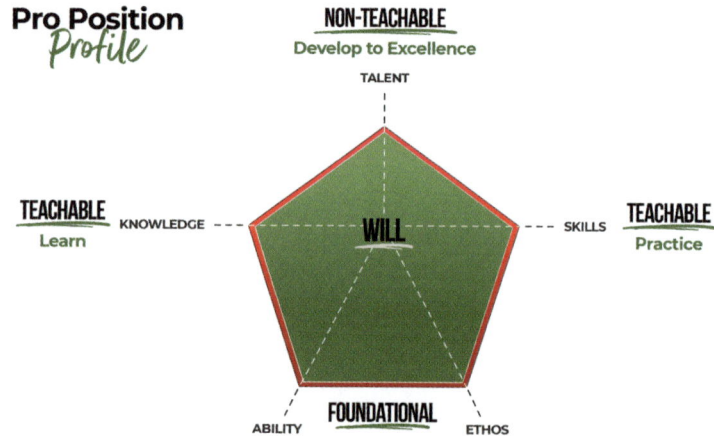

These individuals have demonstrated strong performance in their current roles and have the natural talent to excel. When fully engaged and working to the top of their talent, the value of this human capital is mutually beneficial. The individuals thrive, create positive energy, delight customers, lead with excellence, and serve as a force multiplier of organizational performance.

As individual capital is developed, so do expectations. Pros may have less tolerance for poor leadership, minimal development, and limited growth. They can be more demanding, recognizing the value their human capital brings to the organization. While spending the least amount of time with pros is easy because they are self-sufficient and highly performing, they also represent the most significant opportunity for return on your HCIS investment.

Reflecting on Sarah's opening story, investment allocation is not about giving everyone the same—it is about positioning human capital where it is most likely to thrive and allocating the necessary resources. This concept supports the law of the vital few, also known as Pareto's 80/20 rule. Optimizing the human capital of pros requires continued development and regular check-ins to ensure they remain engaged and challenged.

Although most leaders understand the concept, they often fail to apply it to the company's most significant financial investment—

HUMAN CAPITAL.

Many leaders fundamentally apply the principle in reverse—spending too much time, money, and energy dealing with underperformers, neglecting those who can impact the bottom line, or attempting to share time and resources equally.

Engendering
HIGH-GROWTH ASSETS

In recent years, the U.S. has seen a sharp decline in employee engagement, revealing a fundamental shift in what today's workforce values—and demands. In 2024, only 31% of U.S. employees reported feeling engaged at work, marking a ten-year low (Forbes

Advisory Board). Meanwhile, half of employees report feeling emotionally detached from their employer, and 45% cite burnout driven by organizational change and a lack of support (HR Policy Forum).

This is not just a morale crisis, it is a failure of strategy.

This is where will is vitally important. Organizations operate with outdated assumptions about what drives performance, often relying on short-term incentives while ignoring the deeper forces of human motivation. As Daniel Pink argues in his landmark research and reaffirms in his more recent work, the most powerful drivers of engagement and performance are not extrinsic rewards but **autonomy, mastery, and purpose.**

Great investors think long-term, leveraging the power of compounding returns. Strategic leaders must adopt the same mindset. Sustained workforce engagement—and the innovation, retention, and productivity it fuels—can only be achieved when organizations invest in the internal fuel that drives high performance. This means moving beyond compensation and compliance, and into a new era of motivational design.

FIXED COSTS: TABLE STAKES

Drawing on Herzberg's Two-Factor Theory, we distinguish between hygiene factors (which prevent dissatisfaction) and motivational factors (which enhance engagement). Hygiene factors include basic expectations of market-competitive wages and benefits. However, as the workforce has evolved and human capital is in high demand, some of what were previously considered "nice-to-haves" in today's climate are now strategic imperatives.

Today's workforce expects more than a paycheck. Employees, particularly top performers and emerging leaders, are seeking alignment with organizations that reflect their values, support their well-being, and offer more than transactional employment. Among the rising expectations are flexibility in where and how work gets done, a genuine culture of inclusion where diverse voices are valued, and a visible commitment to social responsibility that extends beyond performative statements. These are no longer differentiators; they are table stakes.

Among these differentiators, flexibility has become one of the most debated. Following the pandemic, which forced many professions into work-from-home situations, flexibility has become a baseline requirement. According to McKinsey, nearly 80% of employees in remote-compatible roles prefer a hybrid arrangement.

For women, flexibility is tied directly to career progression and retention. A 2022 Lean In/McKinsey report found that women leaders are leaving organizations at the highest rate in years, often citing a lack of flexibility as the primary reason. A Future Forum study showed that Black knowledge workers who were allowed to work remotely experienced a 26% increase in job satisfaction.

Flexibility fosters psychological safety for underrepresented talent. **Hygiene is not about perks; it is about foundational trust and credibility**. Based on Herzberg's theory, employers who fail to meet this new baseline risk disengagement, attrition, and reputational decline. Before asking what drives extraordinary engagement, leaders must ensure these foundational expectations are met. Hygiene alone does not create a thriving workforce. It prevents dissatisfaction, but it does not inspire greatness.

HIGH-GROWTH ASSETS: THE MOTIVATIONAL MULTIPLIERS

Motivational factors are more than "soft" elements of culture. They are performance accelerants that foster the psychological conditions in which flow becomes possible and talent becomes transformational.

This is where transactional leadership fails—and individualized leadership begins. When it comes to unlocking discretionary effort, financial incentives and traditional performance management have diminishing returns. What today's workforce craves—and what tomorrow's talent will demand—are deeper sources of motivation.

Organizations must invest in motivational factors to unlock sustained performance, creativity, and commitment—the internal catalysts that fuel initiative, resilience, and excellence. These are the conditions under which high performers not only show up but also show out.

Building on Herzberg's Two-Factor Theory, motivation is not sparked by eliminating dissatisfaction; it is driven by the presence of meaningful, fulfilling work. Motivational factors such as achievement, recognition, responsibility, and growth activate what Herzberg called "true satisfaction"—and what modern behavioral science has expanded on over time.

Daniel Pink's framework, rooted in decades of behavioral science and affirmed by workforce data from McKinsey, LinkedIn, and Gallup, offers a compelling blueprint. In Drive (2009) and his recent work, Pink continues to shift the focus from extrinsic rewards to intrinsic motivators, that which **sustains performance in knowledge-based, purpose-driven environments.**

His research identifies four enduring human needs that, when met, ignite energy, innovation, and long-term commitment. These are not perks. They are strategic design principles for organizations seeking to build engagement, retention, and growth cultures.

Here, Daniel Pink's framework comes fully to life:

- **Autonomy:**
  People do not want to be micromanaged; they want to be trusted. According to the *Harvard Business Review*, employees with autonomy over their work experience greater engagement and significantly less stress. High performers demand the freedom to shape their roles, innovate, and lead without rigid constraints.

- **Mastery:**
  The desire to improve one's skills is a powerful intrinsic motivator. LinkedIn's *2023 Workforce Learning Report* found that 94% of employees would stay longer at a company that invests in their development. High-growth employees view learning as a non-negotiable condition for continued engagement.

- **Purpose:**
  In Pink's words, people want to feel they are working for something larger than themselves. McKinsey's research affirms this: When employees feel connected to a meaningful mission, they are significantly more productive and committed—even in times of uncertainty. The most successful organizations embed purpose into roles, team goals, and enterprise strategy.

- **Recognition:**
  Gallup and Workhuman found that frequent, authentic recognition leads to a 4x increase in engagement. Yet most companies under-deliver. Recognition, when tied to values and visible behaviors, becomes a form of positive reinforcement that shapes culture and retains talent.

These findings reinforce Herzberg's original insights: While hygiene factors are essential for preventing dissatisfaction, they are insufficient on their own. Organizations must intentionally invest in the motivational drivers that matter most to unlock the discretionary effort, creativity, and loyalty of today's workforce.

When organizations treat motivation as a strategic asset, they stop relying on carrots and sticks and start designing conditions for sustainable excellence. This is not about being "soft," but about being smart.

STRATEGIC TALENT IMPLICATIONS

Reflecting on the definition of talent and the intrinsic satisfaction of working in an area of strength, we can see the parallels to Herzberg's, Csikszentmihalyi's, and Pink's research. Data from Gallup's *State of the Global Workplace Report* indicates that **employees who strongly agree they have opportunities to do what they do best are six times more likely to be engaged and three times more likely to stay with their current employer.**

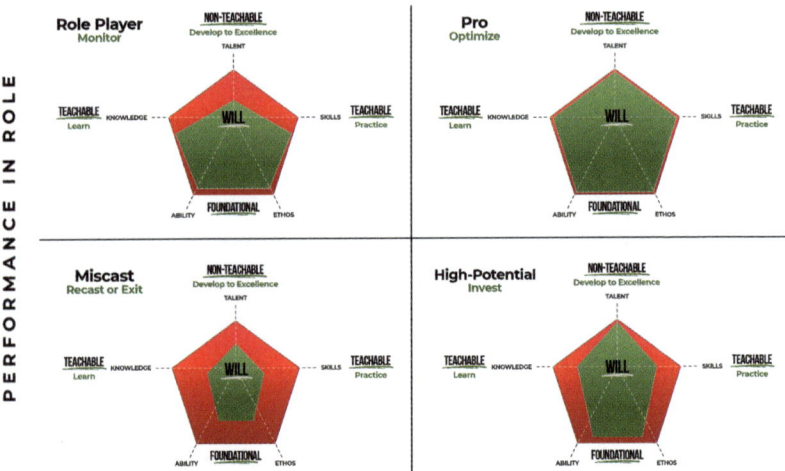

TALENT FOR ROLE

Unlike financial capital, these valuable assets have self-agency and opportunity—they choose to be part of an organization. This elite subset of the HCP brings exponential value to the bottom line. Just as investors diversify portfolios and reinvest in high-performing assets, leaders must identify, develop, and continually nurture high-growth individuals through tailored motivational strategies. Those who do will reap exponential returns—not just in productivity but also in innovation, loyalty, and resilience. Those who do not will continue to lose their most valuable assets to organizations that understand this simple truth: Motivated people outperform managed people every time.

INVESTMENT

From a financial perspective, investing in individual motivation factors yields significant returns. Deloitte's research on workforce engagement shows that **companies with highly engaged employees report 21% higher profitability and 17% higher productivity compared to those with low engagement**. According to SHRM, the cost of replacing a high-performing employee can reach up to 200% of their annual salary, further highlighting the economic rationale for proactive investment in motivation strategies.

Leaders who approach talent management through an investor's lens recognize that their most valuable assets—high-performing individuals—require continuous, personalized investment. Just as sophisticated investors allocate resources to high-yield opportunities rather than simply maintaining baseline returns, organizations must strategically enhance motivation factors to unlock peak performance. In doing so, they create a sustainable HCP, where top talent remains engaged, innovative, and committed to driving long-term success.

When organizations apply resource allocation and invest in their HCP, rather than treating it as a labor burden, they cultivate potential and yield a competitive advantage. The force multiplier that pros represent significantly contributes to yielding bullish returns. The economies of scale realized from investing in a talent portfolio are exponential.

By continuously adjusting human capital allocations, organizations ensure they maximize **the value of every workforce investment.**

....

Conclusion

Winning organizations do not just acquire talent; they cultivate and optimize it over time. Just as a well-balanced financial portfolio requires ongoing assessment and reallocation, a thriving workforce depends on intentional management, strategic investment, and continuous development.

By rebalancing human capital with precision—exiting underperforming assets, monitoring progress, investing in high-growth individuals, and optimizing motivation structures—leaders create an ecosystem where employees flourish and the business gains a sustainable competitive advantage.

The best leaders do not merely react to workforce trends; they shape them by making strategic, forward-looking decisions. Like expert investors, they recognize that long-term success is not about quick fixes, but about consistently allocating resources intelligently. When leaders master this mindset, they unlock the full potential of their teams—and, in turn, their organizations.

CASE STUDY:

Henry Ford West Bloomfield Hospital

The ROI of Allocating for Alignment, Not Just Function

In portfolio theory, rebalancing is not just about redistribution; it is a strategic realignment of assets to maximize returns and minimize unseen risks. The same principle applies to human capital. Organizational success is not built on résumé checklists or standardized staffing models. It is built by placing the right people in the right roles—individuals whose talents, values, and emotional engagement directly align with strategic goals.

Few stories illustrate this better than the transformation led by Gerard van Grinsven, former CEO of Henry Ford West Bloomfield Hospital. Charged with launching a $360 million facility during the depths of the Great Recession, Gerard confronted more than economic headwinds. As a hospitality executive entering healthcare, he also faced deep institutional skepticism. His response? He rebalanced everything.

Instead of hiring based on credentials alone, he selected for innate talent. Every role—from surgeons to administrative assistants—was evaluated using a validated strengths-based assessment to uncover what people were not only capable of doing but uniquely wired to do. Traits like empathy, curiosity, and relationship-building were treated not as "soft skills" but as critical capabilities essential to delivering healing-centered care.

He didn't just hire—he curated. Out of 14,000 applicants, only 1,600 were chosen. Those selected experienced a five-day immersive onboarding focused on purpose, diversity, and connection—long before a single patient entered the building. From day one, the culture was designed to reflect a simple truth: If you treat employees with trust, respect, and dignity, they will do the same for the guests (not "patients") they serve.

He didn't just fill roles—he orchestrated fit. Departments operated as integrated, interdependent teams. Every leader was expected to be visible and accessible, spending time on the floor rather than in meeting rooms. Team talent maps, collaborative coaching, and clearly defined expectations created an environment where performance was not imposed—it was co-owned. Goals were set, refined, and aligned with what employees believed truly mattered.

The results were extraordinary. Within weeks of opening, the hospital captured major market share. Within two years, it became one of the most profitable nonprofit hospitals in the United States—leading its peers in patient satisfaction, clinical outcomes, employee engagement, and operational efficiency. The return on human capital was clear and undeniable.

Rebalancing allocations is not about shifting people. It is about positioning your most valuable asset—your people—where their strengths can be fully activated, supported by a culture that brings out their best, and enabled by systems that amplify success.

This is how you create exponential returns—financial, operational, and reputational.

When you rebalance with purpose, you do not just optimize talent.

You unlock possibility.

IMPLEMENTING
STEP FOUR

I. OVERVIEW & OBJECTIVES
- **Objective**
  Reallocate talent investment, development resources, and leadership attention based on performance, potential, and risk—maximizing ROI on human capital while reducing inefficiencies and organizational drag.

- **Key Message**
  Rebalancing is not about fairness—it's about yield. Just as investors rebalance their portfolios to optimize for growth and risk, leaders must dynamically adjust human capital allocations to unlock value and drive future performance.

- **Mindset Shift**
  "Intestinal fortitude increases when you add science to your gut." Use data to make courageous talent decisions that accelerate performance—even when they challenge legacy assumptions or emotional loyalties.

II. STEP-BY-STEP ACTION PLAN

1. Exit or Recast Underperformers

- **Purpose**
  Address individuals whose performance is persistently low and whose natural talent does not align with role demands.

- **Actions**
  - **Assess Fit:** Confirm that poor performance is not due to training gaps, unclear expectations, or poor management.

  - **Explore Recasting:** If strengths are evident, explore lateral moves or restructured roles that better align with natural capabilities.

  - **Implement Exit Plans:** For persistently misaligned talent, design a dignified and legally compliant exit strategy.

- **Key Message**
  Retaining misaligned talent corrodes culture, slows performance, and diverts investment away from growth.

2. Monitor Talent with Mixed Signals

- **Purpose**
  Identify employees who are performing adequately but may not be in the proper long-term role, or whose engagement or adaptability poses a future risk.

- **Actions**
  - **Create Watch Lists:** Flag individuals with inconsistent feedback or who hover between performance quadrants.
  - **Investigate Context:** Analyze team dynamics, leadership quality, role clarity, and support structures.
  - **Adjust Strategy:** Consider pairing them with complementary team members, adjusting responsibilities, or increasing oversight.

3. Invest Heavily in High-Growth Talent

- **Purpose**
  Accelerate the development of individuals with high natural talent but current performance limitations due to teachable gaps.

- **Actions**
  - **Create Individualized Growth Plans:** Define clear development goals and map a tailored timeline for improvement.
  - **Remove Barriers:** Provide additional tools, coaching, and manager support to reduce ramp-up friction.
  - **Monitor Progress Closely:** Set short-cycle feedback and milestone checkpoints.

- **Key Message**
  This is your "buy low, scale fast" opportunity. When supported strategically, these individuals often produce the highest ROI.

4. Optimize Top Performers

- **Purpose**
  Ensure pros remain engaged, challenged, and retained.

- **Actions**
  - **Create Career Pathing:** Map future roles that stretch capabilities and expand leadership impact.

  - **Recognize & Reward:** Tie compensation, recognition, and visibility to the consistent pros.

  - **Leverage as Mentors:** Deploy them as culture carriers, peer coaches, and internal influencers.

- **Pro Tip**
  Neglecting top performers creates flight risk. They need purpose and growth, not just praise.

5. Reallocate Resources for Strategic ROI

- **Purpose**
  Move budget, manager time, and development opportunities from low-return activities to high-potential segments.

- **Actions**
  - **Shift L&D Budgets:** Prioritize resources for high-growth and high-potential talent over remedial efforts that yield little return.

- **Target High-Impact Roles:** Allocate executive attention to roles and functions with the highest strategic leverage.

- **Align Rewards Systems:** Recalibrate total rewards to reflect actual contribution and forward-looking potential.

- **Key Message**
  You wouldn't keep funding a flatlining asset. The same discipline applies to people investments.

6. Normalize Rebalancing as a Strategic Discipline

- **Purpose**
  Embed rebalancing into leadership culture as a continuous and data-driven business process.

- **Actions**

  - **Educate Leaders:** Train managers to interpret performance/talent/potential data, navigate difficult conversations, and make balanced reallocation decisions.

  - **Integrate into Cadence:** Conduct rebalancing reviews during quarterly talent reviews, succession meetings, and annual planning.

  - **Track Impact:** Measure the performance lift and cultural impact of reallocation decisions over time.

- **Pro Tip**
  Rebalancing is not a one-time correction—it's

an executive habit. Normalize it as a strategic
lever, not a punitive act.

III. TOOLS
www.cynthiabentzenmercer.com/resources

- Human Capital Investment Strategy Framework
- AHC Rebalancing Path Forward
- *Miscast* Position Profile
- *Role Player* Position Profile
- *High Potential* Position Profile
- *Pro* Position Profile

IV. NEXT STEP
With your human capital allocations recalibrated for performance and potential, advance to Step Five: Expand
Options. This next step focuses on building a broader,
higher-quality, and more diverse talent pipeline—ensuring sustainable, long-term growth capacity.

STEP FIVE

EXPAND OPTIONS

The greatest opportunities exist beyond the obvious—only those who are willing to explore will uncover them.

Imagine you're in Las Vegas, standing at the roulette table. You watch as the ball lands on red five times in a row. A man beside you smirks and places his chips on black, thinking it must land on black this time.

However, if you are familiar with probability, you recognize that his logic is flawed. The wheel has no memory; each spin is independent. Nevertheless, time and again, people make decisions based on gut feelings, instincts, and perceived patterns rather than actual data.

Now, here's the real kicker:

BUSINESSES MAKE THE SAME CHOICES EVERY DAY WHEN SELECTING INDIVIDUALS.

Consider how the hiring process typically unfolds. A candidate enters an interview, offers a firm handshake, establishes strong eye contact, and shares a compelling narrative. Immediately, the hiring manager forms a favorable impression of the candidate. They might see a reflection of themselves in the candidate or feel that this person is the right fit for the position.

Months later, the same manager is baffled as this "sure bet" continues to struggle to perform. The issue? They relied on a hunch instead of the odds.

Great investors don't gamble; they analyze. They utilize models, data, and historical performance to forecast future returns. The same principle applies to hiring and promotion.

Predictive validity assessments evaluate the effectiveness of a selection method in predicting future performance. Research indicates that structured interviews and validated assessments of problem-solving ability significantly outperform intuition, résumés, or even years of experience.

Imagine selecting a stock based on the CEO's charisma rather than on actual financial metrics. Many companies engage in this practice when they depend on unstructured interviews or a "gut feeling."

What does this mean for business? **Organizations that utilize validated measures—rather than relying on intuition—create stronger teams, outperform their competitors, and minimize costly hiring mistakes.**

Betting ON GUT INSTINCT

As noted in previous steps, an experienced observer can easily identify natural talent in sports or recognize it in the performing arts. However, sourcing, attracting, and selecting potential talent in business is significantly more challenging. As discussed in Step Two, instincts can be enhanced by focusing on validated metrics. This factor becomes even more crucial when sourcing candidates from outside the organization, where historical observations are unavailable. Without past experience, the human brain quickly attempts to identify other indications of "fit" for the position and the organization.

AFFINITY BIAS

Early in my career, I interviewed a candidate for a senior training role—a position of visibility and influence. As I approached the lobby to greet her, I instinctively took in her appearance: a bold pantsuit, open-toed shoes, and no stockings. In that moment, I had a visceral reaction—not to her qualifications, but to how her attire clashed with the unspoken dress codes I had internalized from working in ultra-conservative environments, where women in leadership wore skirt suits, neutral tones, and closed-toed heels.

I was taken aback—not by her, but by the mental dissonance I experienced. Without even realizing it, I had constructed a mental model of what a "professional woman" should look like, and she did not fit the mold. I am not proud of that reaction. Looking back, I see how my discomfort had nothing to do with her capabilities and everything to do with my own unconscious expectations.

Thankfully, I did not let that fleeting bias guide my decision. I selected her, and she turned out to be exceptional. However, the encounter stuck with me. It was my first real lesson in how easily *affinity bias*—our preference for those who look, act, or think like us—can cloud judgment, even among the most well-intentioned leaders.

Research by Henri Tajfel and John Turner (1997) suggests that people naturally surround themselves with others from their in-group, those who share commonality. This Social Identity Theory of natural grouping occurs based on factors such as race and ethnicity, age, gender, social status, occupation, and religion.

One way in-groups are perpetuated in the workplace is through affinity bias. Neuroscience has found that our brains process approximately 11 million bits of information at any given moment, but we can only handle around 40 bits simultaneously. Affinity bias enables the brain to synthesize information more quickly, facilitating unconscious and immediate assessments of whether someone is a friend or foe.

A study by Northwestern University (2016) found that hiring managers were significantly more likely to engage in informal conversations and express a "gut feeling" of connection with candidates who shared their alma mater, hometown, or hobbies, often leading to more positive impressions.

While most discerning investors would never choose a fund solely based on its catchy name, the CEO's alma mater, or logo, when a candidate resembles, shares a similar background with, or has other relatable characteristics to the hiring leader, the chances of a "good feeling" increase.

HALO EFFECT

Affinity bias can occur independently or in conjunction with the halo effect. When a prospect is interviewing, they put forth their best effort. They arrive dressed in what they believe will make the strongest impression. Their answers are carefully crafted, as they are often anticipated. In general, people present themselves to create a strong first impression.

The halo effect refers to a cognitive bias in which one positive aspect or trait influences the overall judgment of a person, regardless of its actual merit. A pleasant demeanor, a sense of humor, a sharp outfit, or a clear communication style can provide an instant impression of compatibility. Not surprisingly, the "horn effect" can also take place. A candidate's weak handshake, awkwardness, communication style, or even shoes can trigger a single negative impression that is then attributed more broadly.

....

Indirect COSTS

Relying on non-predictive hiring methods, such as gut instinct, relatability, and first impressions, can lead to costly mistakes. As discussed in Step Three, unstructured interviews have low predictive validity (0.22), rendering them ineffective for assessing future job performance. Unsurprisingly, a Career-Builder survey found that 75% of employers admitted to hiring the wrong person.

The financial impact of a bad hire varies widely; among companies that faced a negative impact in the past year, the average cost per bad hire was nearly $17,000. However, this figure may be conservative. Other estimates suggest the cost could be as much as 30% of the employee's annual salary (U.S. Department of Labor) or even as much as $240,000 (Link Humans).

In calculating the cost of a bad hire, what most companies fail to quantify is the financial impact of:

- Lost Productivity
- Lost Clients
- Damaged Reputation with Clients
- Damaged Employer Reputation
- Decreased Teamwork
- Lost Time Supervising a Bad Hire
- Legal Fees

....

Opportunity COSTS

While the cost of a bad hire is significant, missed opportunities are where the HCP is most affected in the long term. Consider all the candidates who had immense human capital and were a good fit for both the role and the organization yet were overlooked. Perhaps the hiring leader did not have a connection or 'affinity' toward the candidate, or they felt negative about their op"affinity" shoes! Alternatively, perhaps, they lacked that immediate wow factor that a less-qualified candidate might have displayed.

The same non-predictive considerations that can lead to a costly hiring decision are also responsible for overlooking the force multiplier that the right human capital can provide. **Unfilled positions** cost the company productivity, sales, service, or revenue, when the hiring leader is holding out for a type instead of taent.

In the current workforce landscape, an organization may not get another chance to hire those candidates it passed over.

TALENTED INDIVIDUALS WHO HAVE BEEN REJECTED FOR A ROLE AT YOUR COMPANY OFTEN TAKE THEIR HUMAN CAPITAL TO YOUR COMPETITOR.

DIVERSIFICATION AS A *Competitive* ADVANTAGE

The more significant opportunity cost occurs when the human capital that was overlooked represented an opportunity to diversify the HCP. Diversification is just as important in human capital investments as it is in financial investments. While most organizations acknowledge this fact, they often find themselves either paralyzed by a lack of competence in strategic diversification or stuck in the belief that strategic diversification necessitates sacrificing performance. Both of these barriers will be addressed.

Beginning with the latter, when organizations apply the same rigor, discipline, and predictive analytics to human capital decisions as they do to financial investments, they make informed choices that are not swayed by superficial biases. Predictive selection methods increase the likelihood of identifying individuals with the highest potential for alignment, performance, and long-term value creation. **As human capital is not confined to any specific background, demographic, or pedigree, this approach leads to a more diversified HCP.**

Diversifying an HCP is not about quotas or absolutes. It is about not limiting the portfolio to just one type of asset and ensuring that the organization's breadth and depth provide a well-rounded worldview, representing the markets and clients served. Just as one would not invest all their financial assets in a single, safe, low-risk asset type, one would not want an HCP that reflects a narrow group, as that would limit insights and innovation. Had PlayStation not diversified its HCP, it would not have gained the increased market share it enjoys today.

When companies incorporate science into their decision-making and rely on more predictive measures of future performance, tendencies such as affinity bias and halo effect are mitigated, resulting in a naturally rich and diverse HCP. The opportunity to cultivate potential and yield a competitive advantage is significant, especially when competitors continue to use unreliable approaches.

- Companies in the top quartile for ethnic and cultural diversity were **36% more likely to outperform** those in the bottom quartile in terms of profitability (McKinsey & Company, 2023).
- Companies in the top quartile for gender diversity on executive teams were **25% more likely to have above-average profitability** than those in the bottom quartile (McKinsey & Company, 2020).
- Firms with female CEOs or CFOs had **higher profitability and lower stock price volatility,** suggesting improved risk management (S&P Global, 2019).

- Companies with greater age diversity in leadership teams showed **higher innovation revenue** (by 19%), as multi-generational teams bring varied insights into prmultigenerationalton Consulting Group, 2021).

- Organizations that leverage multi-generational teams are **30% more likely to becmultigenerationalders** over the next five years (Deloitte, 2020).

INVESTING IN UNTAPPED *Potential*

Recounting the AHC in Step Two reminds us of the attributes of human capital. We have established that ability and ethos (cultural alignment) are essential requirements. Additionally, we noted that knowledge and skills can be taught. This suggests that only the minimum or requisite knowledge and skills necessary for performing in the role should be required, as gaps can be bridged through training and development.

AHC Rebalancing Path Forward

Source: Copyright 2023, Talent Plus® Lincoln, Nebraska.

With that as a foundation, the most significant opportunity for increasing the probability of selecting a high potential or pro lies in ensuring that there is strong talent for the role. In other words, if there is a bet to be placed or a risk to be taken, our odds of success increase exponentially when we select the non-teachable attributes and fill the teachable gaps with education. This approach dramatically widens the pool from which we source talent when not limited by arbitrary non-predictive criteria of years of experience and expertise.

Consider Frank McEwen, a British art collector who arrived in what is now Zimbabwe during the 1950s. He had spent years in Europe's elite art circles, immersed in the works of Picasso, Matisse, and the avant-garde. However, he never expected to discover some of the world's most breathtaking sculptures—not in Paris or London, but in the remote villages of Africa.

These artists were not classically trained, nor did they adhere to European techniques. They were farmers and laborers—individuals whose extraordinary talent had gone unrecognized beyond their local communities. However, when McEwen provided them with materials and opportunities, they created sculptures that rivaled those in the world's greatest museums.

Although the Zimbabwean sculptors lacked formal credentials, they possessed a natural instinct for form, movement, and storytelling through stone. Given the right conditions, they flourished.

Organizations frequently focus on candidates with prestigious degrees, polished résumés, and proven track records. However, the real competitive advantage lies in looking beyond appearances and using predictive measures to inform decisions.

Companies should adopt a similar mindset. Rather than concentrating solely on choosing candidates based on experience, they should invest in potential. **Instead of filling positions with** "safe" candidates, they should seek individuals with unique perspectives, creativity, and resilience who can shape the future rather than merely conform to the present.

Every individual has inherent greatness and talent. By mastering the ability to see beyond what is immediately visible, you can cultivate an unstoppable workforce prepared to achieve excellence.

....

REFINE SELECTION *Criteria*

The financial benefits of integrating diverse human capital into an organization are evident. However, most companies encounter the main challenge of identifying and attracting unique, untapped talent ahead of their competitors.

Harvard Business Review research found that women apply to jobs only if they meet 100% of the listed criteria, whereas men apply when they meet only 60%. This is not a matter of confidence or impostor syndrome; it stems from how different populations interpret job qualifications and expectations. Many underrepresented candidates—particularly women and minorities—view qualifications as strict requirements rather than guidelines, which effectively screens them out before they even enter the talent pipeline.

This self-elimination problem is compounded by legacy hiring practices prioritizing experience over predictive performance indicators, such as problem-solving ability, adaptability, and leadership potential. **As companies expand their talent pools externally, adjusting qualification criteria to emphasize potential over traditional experience-based metrics can unlock a new category of high-potential talent.**

When working with an investment planner, one of the first steps after setting goals is establishing the criteria for selecting a fund. The same principle applies to selecting human capital. Before a leader can begin sourcing, it is essential to clarify what they are looking for in the position.

Given the predictive validity of different measures, consider the following when establishing selection criteria for a role:

- **Minimum Knowledge and Skills**
Organizations limit themselves when they mandate a specific educational background that is unnecessary for performing the essential functions of the role. Relying on outdated criteria, such as a college degree, has limited validity in predicting future performance (0.10). Of course, this is unrelated to licensing requirements or positions requiring a degree, such as a medical doctor.

- **Years of Experience**
Employers typically require a certain number of years of experience. However, years of experience have low validity in predicting future performance ($r = 0.08$). Arbitrarily enforcing years of experience for a specific role restricts the organization from pursuing candidates with transferable natural talent. For instance, a former travel agent might be an ideal candidate for a medical assistant position in a clinic office. A server in a restaurant could also be an outstanding customer service representative.

- **Talent for Role**
The talent required for the position, which serves as the most predictive indicator of future performance when using a structured or behavior-based assessment ($r = 0.50$), is often not clearly defined in the selection criteria. This presents a significant opportunity to enhance the structured interview for the role.

It is vital to take time to document the non-teachable attributes that are most critical for success in the position. Does the role require creativity, persuasion, influential communication, conflict resolution, positivity, etc.? Select natural talent; teach the skills and knowledge!

Given the above points, job advertisements should better reflect this predictive selection process by removing arbitrary, non-predictive requirements. Although not applicable to all industries, those that are highly regulated, such as healthcare, must also ensure that their job descriptions reflect the revised selection criteria.

....

EXISTING ASSET *Opportunities*

Many organizations instinctively look outward when sourcing talent for future roles, assuming that the best candidates must be external hires. However, research consistently shows that companies often overlook their greatest assets—the talent already within their workforce. Before launching extensive external search efforts, organizations should first apply the same talent-focused approach internally, ensuring they are not missing opportunities to develop and elevate their existing employees.

Internal mobility has proven to be a competitive advantage. A LinkedIn *Global Talent Trends* report found that employees who make an internal move are 64% more likely to stay with a company after three years compared to those who remain in the same role. Furthermore, a study by the Wharton School of Business revealed that external hires often take longer to ramp up, perform worse in the first two years, and cost significantly more—yet they are still more likely to leave within three years than those promoted from within.

Assuming the AHC process penetrates sufficiently deep within the organization, sourcing begins with existing potential. Beyond identifying internal candidates, companies must also ensure that they create an environment where internal mobility is not only possible but encouraged and supported.

A McKinsey study found that 70% of employees want career development opportunities, yet fewer than 30% feel their organization provides clear paths for advancement. Without intentional investment in upskilling, reskilling, and cross-functional exposure, companies risk stagnation and disengagement, losing talent that could have been their next great leaders.

The most effective organizations apply the same principles to internal talent as they do to external recruitment: strategic sourcing, relationship-building, and targeted development. They utilize data-driven talent assessments, AI-powered internal marketplaces, and transparent career pathing to match employees with opportunities. They empower managers to act as talent scouts within the organization, identifying high-potential employees and advocating for their professional development and growth. They foster a culture where seeking new challenges within the company is seen as a strength, not a betrayal.

While no single source prescribes the exact ratio for all industries, research from *Harvard Business Review* (HBR), Gartner, LinkedIn, and McKinsey support the idea that **a strong internal pipeline (around 60%–75% of roles filled internally) leads to better retention and engagement, while a controlled influx of external hires (20%–40%) fosters innovation and prevents stagnation.**

CASE STUDY:

FedEx

The ROI of Growing Your Own

During his 23-year career at FedEx, Reginald Mebane advanced from loading trucks on the night shift to becoming Chief Operating Officer of a $2 billion business unit. His journey exemplifies what happens when an organization treats people not as positions to be filled, but as *investments to be developed.*

Mebane's rise reflects the disciplined application of human capital strategy—centered on internal mobility, leadership cultivation, and equity. His story underscores a central truth of the HCIS framework: When companies invest intentionally in people, they outperform the market while building cultures of loyalty, excellence, and long-term return.

From its inception, FedEx was grounded in Fred Smith's People-Service-Profit (PSP) philosophy—a business model predicated on the idea that if you take care of your people, performance and profits will follow. This was not a slogan; it was operational doctrine. Every major decision was evaluated for its impact on employees.

To act on that belief, FedEx pioneered early talent practices, including:

- Assessment-based hiring and promotion

- Structured internal mobility pathways
- Targeted leadership identification and development

FedEx treated potential as a measurable, developable asset. Talent reviews were not solely about tenure; they were about observed capability, values alignment, and growth trajectory. Reginald Mebane's progression—from ramp manager to COO—isn't an anomaly; it's a product of this disciplined approach.

At Step Five in the HCIS framework—Expand Options—leaders are challenged to build optionality into their workforce strategy. At FedEx, this didn't require widening the external funnel. It meant looking inward and multiplying future possibilities by cultivating the people already inside the organization.

Here's how FedEx operationalized this strategy:

- **Mobility Over Market Searches**
  Rather than defaulting to external hires, FedEx prioritized internal promotion. Mebane's rise was not incidental—it was the result of a systemic talent pipeline designed to identify and advance high-potential individuals from frontline roles. Leadership is built, not bought. Mebane graduated from the FedEx Leadership Institute, an internal academy focused on building servant leaders equipped with operational

acumen and cultural fluency. At FedEx, training wasn't an add-on—it was foundational.

- **Culture as Strategy**
  Employees routinely went above and beyond—fueling planes, hand-delivering packages, and standing in airport lines—not because they were told to, but because they felt a sense of ownership. That discretionary effort came from feeling seen, supported, and integral to the mission.

- **Equity as Expansion**
  FedEx created real career ladders for people from all walks of life, decades before DEI became mainstream. The company's promotion philosophy was based on potential, not pedigree. That widened its talent pool and deepened its leadership bench.

Leadership development at FedEx wasn't reactive; it was embedded in the operating model. Learning, coaching, and mentoring were standard expectations—not reserved perks. Mebane's career trajectory was powered by early identification, ongoing feedback, and structured growth opportunities—all designed to align human capital with enterprise needs.

While FedEx actively pursued market expansion, one of its most powerful and underappreciated levers was its internal leadership pipeline. By believing in the upward mobility of frontline employees, the organization unlocked innovation, fostered emotional engagement, and reduced turnover—all while ensuring cultural consistency through cycles of change.

Outcomes & Strategic Impact

- **Resilient Talent Bench**
  Ready-now leaders ensured continuity, speed, and alignment during business shifts.

- **Increased Loyalty, Lower Turnover**
  Investing in internal growth created emotional investment and organizational stickiness.

- **Sustainable Competitive Advantage**
  The PSP philosophy translated into shareholder value and operational excellence.

- **Culture of Discretionary Effort**
  Employees consistently exceeded expectations because they felt they mattered.

- **Measured Inclusion**
  The company operationalized internal equity long before it was a compliance issue.

Expanding your options does not always mean looking outward. It means *building* capacity inward—by developing, retaining, and promoting the talent you already have. FedEx's long-term performance has not been luck. It is the result of deliberate, sustained investment in people.

Mebane's story reminds us that when human capital is treated as an appreciating asset, its returns are evident on every line of the business, through loyalty, innovation, and competitive resilience.

Source LIKE A VENTURE CAPITALIST

Many of the most promising candidates, particularly those from underrepresented backgrounds, are not actively seeking jobs. McKinsey research indicates that 70% of the global workforce is considered "passive talent," meaning they are currently employed and not actively seeking new roles. However, they would be open to the right opportunity. Within this group, diverse professionals and those in leadership pipelines are even less likely to be in active job markets, as they often lack the sponsorship or recruitment outreach that connects them to higher-level opportunities.

This is where sourcing becomes a competitive advantage. Unlike traditional recruitment, which relies on applicants coming forward, sourcing involves identifying, researching, and engaging high-potential talent before they are actively seeking opportunities. The most forward-thinking organizations utilize data-driven sourcing strategies, leveraging AI-powered talent platforms, industry networks, and internal referrals to construct talent pipelines encompassing overlooked or underutilized candidates.

The urgency for organizations to refine their sourcing strategies is growing. As outlined in Step One, demographic shifts in the labor force indicate that women, minorities, and multigenerational employees will be in even higher demand in the coming decades. A Korn Ferry study projects that by 2030, the global talent shortage could reach 85 million people, with companies that fail to attract diverse candidates facing severe workforce gaps. **Companies that move first in establishing sourcing pipelines, reducing rigid job criteria, and building relationships with passive talent will gain a significant competitive advantage in the war for high-caliber, diverse leadership.**

Ultimately, the most forward-looking organizations will stop merely selecting talent from active applicants and start discovering talent that is not yet in the market. By expanding selection criteria and proactively sourcing diverse candidates, businesses can unlock hidden pools of high-potential talent, creating a workforce that is not only more representative but also more capable, innovative, and resilient in the face of an evolving labor market.

PROACTIVE SOURCING

Just as venture capitalists actively seek investment opportunities through various channels, so should every leader. Proactive sourcing must not be limited to the recruitment department. Every leader should source talent through:

- **Referrals:**
Talent knows talent. One sourcing strategy is encouraging current employees to refer individuals to the organization. The caution is to encourage referrals of those with diverse backgrounds. As noted in the Sony example, birds of a feather tend to flock with their kind.

- **Networking:**
Building relationships is the strongest source of expanding the human capital pool. However, networking must be intentionally diverse. Leaders must attend conferences and events that expose them to diverse audiences and perspectives.

- **Online Platforms & Database:**
Utilizing platforms like LinkedIn to build relationships is crucial for expanding a global network. Leaders should be encouraged to build a strong online presence.

- **High Schools, Trade Schools & Universitie:**
Partnering with local high schools and trade schools is an excellent way to introduce the organization. Working with high schools, particularly those in underserved areas, can foster industry awareness and interest. Historically Black Colleges and Universities (HBCUs) are another often untapped source of human capital.

- **Daily Interactions:**
Consider that the organization's next top performer could be anywhere. The waitress with a warm disposition and the ability to anticipate needs, the organized, helpful, and dependable grocery store clerk, and the manager at the local gym—each of these individuals could be a strong candidate for a position in a completely different industry. Leaders should always be looking for human capital that would complement the portfolio.

Adopting a venture capitalist mindset, companies should continuously pursue the next human capital investment and consistently source talent, irrespective of current openings.

While sourcing encompasses broad efforts to fill pipelines, prospecting is a strategic approach emphasizing high-value or unique talent among candidates who may not actively seek a job change.

PROSPECTING *Potential*

Prospecting is a more specialized and proactive form of sourcing, often employed for niche or high-impact roles, particularly in executive search, sports, entertainment, and specialized industries. **Prospecting involves building deeper relationships and gathering competitive intelligence, often requiring identifying candidates who may not be listed on traditional job platforms.**

Major League Baseball is one of the best examples of prospecting and leading with potential. Some of the greatest players were discovered far from traditional talent pipelines. Take Shohei Ohtani from Japan, Ronald Acuña Jr. from Venezuela, and Fernando Tatís Jr. from the Dominican Republic—each was scouted in areas that, decades ago, might not have been on every team's radar.

This was not by accident. There was an intentional and strategic approach to recognizing the value of talent over experience. Major League Baseball teams have invested in several significant changes. **First, they expanded their talent search** beyond American high school and college recruits. Prospecting talent from new and previously untapped markets granted access to human capital that would have otherwise been overlooked.

They invested in scouting networks, recruiting specialists dedicated to uncovering unrealized potential. This enabled the teams to source talent beyond what was immediately apparent.

Furthermore, **they redefined what a "prospect" looks like**. Recognizing the non-teachable talents that contribute to making world-class ball players, the teams sought will, ability, ethos, and potential. They established academies to impart knowledge and skills. This was perhaps the most galvanizing change.

THE MLB REALIZED THAT EXCEPTIONAL TALENT COULD EMERGE ANYWHERE, BUT ONLY IF YOU'RE WILLING TO LOOK FOR IT.

The same principle applies in organizations. Too often, companies recruit from the same elite universities, industries, or networks. However, the best companies and most innovative thinkers do not always follow a traditional path.

DEVELOPING A TALENT BENCH

The key difference between **sourcing** and **prospecting** lies in the required depth of relationship-building. While sourcing focuses on identifying and engaging individuals who are actively or passively seeking new opportunities, **prospecting** involves proactively cultivating relationships with high-potential talent, often before they even consider a transition.

Because prospecting requires developing a compelling reason for individuals to engage, it is inherently a longer-term strategy that prioritizes relationship-building over immediate hiring needs. A structured talent bench strategy can be a powerful complement to succession planning, ensuring that organizations have strong talent connections in place before a critical need arises, much like strong financial advisors are constantly vigilant for the next promising investment opportunity.

When an opportunity arises, the organization has already established an emotional connection and a foundation of trust, giving it a competitive advantage in influencing top talent to join.

Just as baseball teams establish academies in Latin America

or scout talent in the Japanese leagues, businesses should expand their recruiting strategies to include unconventional backgrounds, non-traditional career paths, and untapped talent pools. They should place big bets on raw talent while teaching the rest.

....

HEDGING YOUR *Bets*

An increased risk is associated with the unknown when attracting and selecting from outside the organization. A significant portion of that risk is mitigated by using predictive assessments. However, an additional risk when expanding an HCP, which emphasizes strong potential and raw natural talent, is the lack of knowledge and skills that must be developed to achieve peak performance.

To ensure performance enablement, at a macro level, leaders should:

- **Provide clear success frameworks:**
  Talent thrives when expectations are transparent and well defined. Define what high performance looks like and provide structured guidance on achieving it.

- **Invest in tools & resources**
  Even the most capable individuals need the right environment to excel. This includes access to learning opportunities, cutting-edge technology, mentorship, and peer collaboration.

- **Normalize real-time feedback**
  Performance should not be measured solely on an annual basis. Frequent, constructive, and data-backed

feedback ensures employees can course-correct, grow, and stay engaged.

Natural ability does not automatically translate to high performance. Talented individuals need structure, resources, and feedback to truly excel. Too many companies hire high-potential individuals and then assume they will "figure it out." This is a costly mistake.

ACCELERATING HUMAN CAPITAL

When organizations commit to hiring raw talent—selecting individuals based on their innate potential rather than polished credentials—they must also commit to building the infrastructure that enables those individuals to succeed. Talent without the necessary skills or knowledge is like an uncut diamond: valuable, but unrealized. That's where three essential development strategies come into play: **onboarding, mentorship, and structured development paths.** These are not "nice to haves"—they are foundational investments that unlock the full value of your HCP.

Onboarding

A well-structured and strategically designed onboarding process is the first and most crucial step in converting raw talent into performance. When onboarding is done right, it compresses the time it takes for a new employee to contribute meaningfully, while embedding them into the culture and mission of the organization. Research from Brandon Hall Group shows that companies with strong onboarding programs see an 82% improvement in new hire retention and a 70% increase in productivity. But effective onboarding is far more than orientation checklists and paperwork. It's about clarity—ensuring that new hires know what success looks like in their role. It's about immersion—introducing not just policies, but the unwritten norms, values, and rhythms that define how the organization works. And it's about connection—creating space for relationship-building from the very start. For individuals hired based on potential, a deliberate onboarding process bridges the gap between raw ability and applied performance.

Mentorship

Once onboarded, high-potential employees need more than technical training—they need guided access to the relational and cultural knowledge that enables them to succeed within your unique environment. That's where mentorship becomes indispensable. A Deloitte study found that employees with mentors are five times more likely to be promoted and report significantly higher job satisfaction. When new hires are paired with seasoned team members who understand the business, culture, and politics of the organization, they gain not only knowledge but access. Mentors accelerate the learning curve, help navigate challenges, and foster belonging. This is particularly important for individuals who may lack formal experience but have been selected for their potential. Mentorship transforms potential into progress. It creates a support structure that validates the organization"s investment in the individual while giving the individual a trusted resource to lean on, learn from, and grow with.

Structured Development Path

Highly talented individuals are not satisfied with simply performing well—they want to grow, evolve, and make an impact. If that pathway isn't visible, they'll look elsewhere. According to LinkedIn's *Workforce Learning Report*, 94% of employees say they would stay at a company longer if it invested in their career development. A structured development path is a clear indication that the organization recognizes potential and is committed to nurturing it. This means more than offering occasional training sessions. It includes defined growth trajectories, ongoing learning opportunities, stretch assignments, and meaningful performance milestones. High-potential employees thrive when they can connect today's work to tomorrow's possibilities. Structured development pathways help individuals envision a future within the company, rather than using it as a stepping stone to someplace else.

STRATEGIC IMPLICATION

Remember, individuals have the agency to decide where they invest their human capital. The most talented people are not just seeking income; they are looking for outcomes—growth, challenge, and purpose. If you do not invest in their ambition, they will take their potential to a competitor who will. By designing effective onboarding experiences, mentorship programs, and structured development paths, organizations significantly increase the likelihood that potential will become performance, and performance will lead to retention.

In tight labor markets, expanding options through thoughtful development design creates access to broader and more diverse talent pools. And when you treat talent acquisition and development as an investment, rather than a transaction, you position your organization not just to compete, but to outperform. These strategies are what turn raw talent into realized value, creating a pipeline of future-ready leaders and unlocking exponential returns across your HCP.

Conclusion

The greatest investors do not gamble; they assess risk, leverage data, and diversify their portfolios. This same approach must apply to human capital investment. Companies that rely on gut instinct, affinity bias, and surface-level assessments when making hiring decisions are taking a risk with their future. In contrast, organizations that adopt a venture capitalist mindset—expanding their talent pipelines, using predictive analytics, and prioritizing potential over pedigree—gain a significant strategic advantage.

By applying structured sourcing and prospecting strategies, leveraging predictive measures, and offering robust onboarding, mentorship, and development programs, companies can identify hidden talent, accelerate their growth, and cultivate a workforce that fosters a sustained competitive advantage. The opportunity cost of neglecting top talent is too significant to overlook.

To stay ahead of the competition, businesses must cease relying on instincts and begin investing in human capital with the same rigor they apply to financial assets. However, HCIS is not a one-time initiative but a long-term, strategic endeavor that demands discipline, resilience, and unwavering commitment from leadership. Organizations that succeed in embedding HCIS into their DNA recognize that investing in human capital is not merely a function of HR—it is a core business strategy that directly impacts innovation, agility, and long-term profitability.

No matter how elegant or well reasoned an HCIS may be, its long-term value hinges on one critical capability: the organization's ability to continuously forecast, monitor, and adjust.

STEP SIX IS THE DYNAMIC ENGINE THAT KEEPS THE STRATEGY ALIVE AND RESPONSIVE.

It represents the shift from static planning to a disciplined, intelligence-driven model of human capital stewardship, where human capital decisions evolve in lockstep with business realities.

IMPLEMENTING
STEP FIVE

I. OVERVIEW & OBJECTIVES

- **Objective**
  Broaden the talent pipeline by adopting a data-driven, venture capital–inspired approach to sourcing and selecting high-potential individuals, both internally and externally.

- **Key Message**
  The highest-yield talent investments often come from unconventional sources. Expanding your talent options requires you to look beyond the obvious, overcome embedded biases, and invest in future value—before it's fully realized.

- **Mindset Shift**
  Stop playing defense. Great leaders don't just evaluate available talent—they go out and find it. Expanding options is about proactive sourcing and prospecting, not reactive hiring.

II. STEP-BY-STEP ACTION PLAN

1. Redefine and Clarify Selection Criteria

- **Purpose**
  Ensure you are selecting for future performance, not just résumé pedigree or surface-level fit.

- **Actions**
  - Prioritize Predictive Attributes
    - o Distinguish between minimum requirements (skills, credentials) and differentiators (natural talent, adaptability, learning agility).
  - Deconstruct the Role
    - o Identify which attributes are teachable vs. innate.
  - Update Job Descriptions
    - o Remove rigid degree or experience requirements that exclude high-potential but nontraditional candidates.
- **Pro Tip**
  Build profiles around "what it takes to win" in the role—not what looks good on paper.

2. Implement Structured, Data-Driven Selection Processes

- **Purpose**
  Reduce bias and improve the predictive validity of hiring decisions.
- **Actions**
  - Use Structured Interviews
    - o Ask the same role-relevant, behavior-based questions to every candidate.
    - o Score responses using defined rubrics.

- Incorporate Validated Assessments
  - o Use tools (e.g., Hogan, Predictive Index, Talent Plus) that measure key traits linked to role success.
- Diversify Interview Panels
  - o Broaden perspectives and reduce groupthink.

- **Key Message**
  Gut decisions are gambling. Structured decisions are investing.

3. Develop Proactive Internal and External Sourcing Strategies

- **Purpose**
  Build a diverse, high-value pipeline before you need it.

- **Actions**
  - Internal Sourcing
    - o Identify internal high-potential talent in overlooked roles.
    - o Launch targeted internal mobility programs.
    - o Incentivize leaders to surface and sponsor hidden talent.
  - External Sourcing
    - o Cultivate passive candidate networks.
    - o Engage talent communities beyond traditional channels.

o   Leverage employee referrals with diversity incentives.

- **Venture Capital Analogy**
  Top venture capitalists don't wait for pitch decks to hit their desk—they scout talent early and build relationships over time.

4. Expand Sourcing Channels and Remove Structural Barriers

- **Purpose**
  Cast a wider net to reach high-value candidates who may not come through traditional pipelines.

- **Actions**
  - **Partner with Diverse Institutions:** Engage HBCUs, women's colleges, trade schools, and community networks.

  - **Use Technology Tools:** Leverage AI-enabled sourcing platforms, skills marketplaces, and predictive talent databases.

  - **Eliminate Unnecessary Filters:** Reevaluate degree requirements and rigid experience minimums.

- **Key Message**
  Exclusionary filters cost you innovation. Inclusion creates strategic differentiation.

5. Enhance Onboarding, Mentorship, and Early Development

- **Purpose**

Accelerate value creation by ensuring expanded talent options are successfully integrated and supported.

- **Actions**
  - **Design Strategic Onboarding:** Focus on cultural immersion, relationship-building, and performance clarity.
  - **Establish Mentorship Networks:** Pair new talent with mentors to facilitate early success.
  - **Launch Development Sprints:** Offer rapid, high-impact development in the first 90 days to shorten time-to-contribution.
- **Pro Tip**
  First impressions shape retention and performance. Early support is a multiplier.

6. Track and Optimize the ROI of Sourcing Strategies

- **Purpose**
  Treat sourcing as an investment function—track performance and returns.
- **Actions**
  - Monitor Key Metrics:
    - Time-to-fill
    - Quality of hire (first-year performance ratings)

o   Retention and promotion velocity

o   Diversity of candidate pools

o   Quality of candidate sourcing tools

— **Conduct Funnel Analysis:** Measure conversion rates at each stage to identify where high-potential candidates are lost.

— **Test and Refine:** Continuously experiment with sourcing channels and messaging strategies.

- **Key Message**
  Every talent strategy is a hypothesis—test, measure, and iterate.

III. TOOLS
www.cynthiabentzenmercer.com/resources

- Human Capital Investment Strategy Framework
- AHC Rebalancing Path Forward

IV. NEXT STEP
With a broader, higher-quality pipeline now in place, proceed to Step Six: Forecast & Adjust. This final step ensures your human capital strategy remains agile and responsive to shifting market conditions, organizational goals, and performance realities.

STEP SIX

FORECAST & ADJUST

Investing in human capital is an endurance sport played on an unpredictable field.

One of the most memorable workforce planning failures was Target's entry into Canada in 2013.

When the company launched its expansion, it underestimated the complexities of staffing its stores, resulting in severe operational issues that ultimately contributed to its downfall.

To launch 124 stores within two years, Target Canada hired thousands of employees in a short time frame. However, many were rushed into positions with minimal training, which left them unprepared to handle customer needs, manage stock, and operate point-of-sale systems. Due to forecasting errors, stores were either overstocked or severely understocked on key items. Employees with limited experience in troubleshooting such challenges were unable to adequately respond to customer inquiries or restock in-demand products quickly enough.

Store managers scrambled to adjust schedules, often leading to staff shortages during peak hours and overstaffing during slow periods. This inconsistency caused long checkout lines, empty shelves, and frustrated customers. With employees feeling overwhelmed and unprepared, service levels deteriorated quickly.

Customer dissatisfaction led to lower-than-expected revenue, making it nearly impossible for Target Canada to recoup its initial investment. The company's inability to meet basic customer expectations tarnished its image. By 2015, just two years after its ambitious launch, Target Canada closed all 133 stores, incurring a $5.4 billion loss and laying off over 17,000 employees.

This case exemplifies why HCIS is not a one-time effort but an ongoing process that must adapt to changing business demands. Even the most well-funded expansion can fail if workforce planning does not anticipate future talent needs and adjust in real-time.

Dynamic FORECASTING

At its core, Forecast & Adjust is about building agility into the system. It ensures that talent plans are not filed away after annual reviews but actively revisited, challenged, and refined. This requires regular workforce planning reviews—ideally conducted monthly or quarterly—by a cross-functional group of leaders, including HR, finance, strategy, and business unit executives. These reviews serve as strategic checkpoints to assess whether talent investments are aligned with current needs and future direction. They provide visibility into planned or emerging role shifts, performance trends, succession readiness, and risk exposure.

Central to this step is the practice of dynamic forecasting. Business strategies shift, market forces evolve, and organizational priorities change. Human capital forecasting must follow suit. Through real-time data and scenario modeling, organizations can anticipate emerging talent gaps, assess workforce supply and demand under different conditions, and proactively manage risks before they materialize. For example, if a pro in a critical role becomes a known flight risk and no immediate successor is in place, it becomes a red flag for that role and the broader pipeline strategy. These predictive insights enable faster, smarter decisions—whether to accelerate development, tap internal mobility, or adjust external hiring plans.

WORKFORCE *Planning*

Building on talent, flight, and depth risk assessments from Step Three, which provide insight at the incumbent level, the workforce plan anticipates needs based on specific positions.

Regardless of the industry, there is an opportunity to identify the most vital positions for operational consistency. Furthermore, aside from unexpected disruptive events, such as tornadoes, earthquakes, and pandemics, trends and patterns are generally identifiable in the data. Implementing a rigorous workforce planning process enables organizations to prepare for downturns and scale up during periods of high volume.

Without strategic workforce planning, companies fall into a vicious cycle of reactionary hiring and layoffs, leading to instability that erodes trust, damages employer branding, and hampers long-term performance. Without a workforce plan in place, organizations frequently overhire during periods of growth, only to cut jobs when budgets tighten, creating a pattern that employees can predict and dread.

One of the most significant threats to the integrity of an HCIS is crisis hiring—when leaders, under pressure to fill open roles quickly, bypass strategic talent criteria and settle for short-term fixes. This reactive approach often leads to compromised quality, cultural misalignment, and increased turnover, undermining the long-term value that the HCIS is designed to create. Crisis hiring also signals a breakdown in proactive workforce planning; it reflects a system that isn't anticipating needs or preparing successors and one that lacks the resilience to absorb even routine attrition without disruption.

In many companies, a particular time of year triggers widespread anxiety as employees brace for the next annual round of layoffs. This fuels uncertainty and disengagement, leading to the loss of institutional knowledge and critical talent, which further deepens instability. Then, as business demands rebound, these same organizations find themselves scrambling to staff up again, often under immense pressure and with diminished employer appeal due to their reputation for volatility.

The result?

A reactive, short-term mindset that undermines long-term workforce stability, disrupts productivity, and drives up costs. **According to a *Harvard Business Review* study, the hidden costs of layoffs—such as lost productivity, weakened morale,** and damage to employer reputation—often outweigh the immediate financial benefits, making mass reductions a costly and shortsighted solution.

Despite its simplicity, research shows that many organizations lack a comprehensive workforce plan that is routinely monitored, stress-tested, and updated to align with business cycles. Instead of proactively managing talent pipelines, they rely on crisis-driven decision-making, failing to anticipate future workforce needs or strategically invest in internal mobility, reskilling, and retention efforts.

Organizations that commit to long-term workforce planning avoid the destabilizing swings of hiring and firing cycles, ensuring that talent investments are aligned with sustainable growth. The challenge for leadership is clear: Move beyond short-term fixes and embrace a deliberate, data-driven approach to human capital—one that builds agility without sacrificing stability and resilience without compromising trust.

WORKFORCE PLANNING METRICS

A 2023 McKinsey study found that high-growth organizations with strategic workforce planning reduced hiring gaps by 40%, minimizing productivity losses. At a minimum, a workforce plan should include the following data pertaining to critical positions (those essential for operational continuity):

Expected Growth/Decline in Department
Understanding business growth trends is essential in forecasting talent needs. Organizations experiencing rapid expansion in sales, product demand, or market expansion must proactively hire before the workload strains productivity. Conversely, anticipating market downturns, automation-driven efficiencies, or restructuring enables

organizations to gradually scale back hiring or reskill employees rather than resorting to sudden layoffs. This data should include seasonality, as those trends are generally easy to predict.

Turnover Rate (Historical & Projected)

High turnover rates lead to increased recruitment costs and productivity losses. Analyzing historical turnover trends helps predict future staffing needs. If turnover consistently exceeds industry benchmarks, workforce planning must address the underlying causes, such as compensation, engagement, and career growth.

Average Tenure

Understanding how long employees typically stay in a role helps predict vacancies and succession planning needs. If the average tenure is short (1-2 years), the organization may need continuous hiring cycles. If it is long (five years or more), hiring may focus more on leadership succession and skill development.

Open Positions

Tracking vacant roles and hiring trends allows businesses to address gaps proactively. If open positions remain unfilled for extended periods, it may indicate a talent shortage or inefficiencies in the recruitment process.

Time to Fill

Measuring how long it takes to hire directly impacts business productivity. A lengthy hiring process can lead to workload strain, disengagement, and lost revenue.

Target Hiring Date

Defining optimal hiring timelines ensures that businesses hire ahead of demand, rather than reacting to talent shortages. Organizations should plan hiring months in advance for high-demand roles, especially in technical or specialized fields.

Training & Development Requirements
If the position requires a lengthy onboarding and training period before assuming the role, this must be factored into the hire date.

....

Governance

Governance ensures that talent decisions are made within the context of enterprise-wide priorities, rather than in isolation. Leaders are empowered with data and accountability to make informed choices about promotions, redeployments, and high-potential designations. Just as importantly, talent outcomes are compared to forecasts—analyzing where predictions held and where they fell short. This type of calibration enhances forecasting accuracy over time and converts missed targets into strategic learning opportunities.

A cross-functional team of leaders should review the workforce plan monthly to ensure it remains aligned with ongoing organizational shifts, such as changes in strategy, market conditions, budget adjustments, or team restructuring. This regular cadence not only keeps the plan current but also reinforces shared accountability across functions for talent decisions. Cross-functional involvement allows for broader visibility into talent supply and demand, surfacing early indicators of risk, overlap, or opportunity that might otherwise be missed in a siloed review.

Regular workforce planning reviews act as a guardrail against this kind of reactive behavior. They provide a forum to anticipate vacancies, track succession depth, and proactively discuss internal mobility options before gaps become urgent. When done well, these reviews embed the HCIS into the operational rhythm of the business—ensuring that talent decisions remain intentional, data-informed, and future-focused, even in the face of shifting priorities or short-term pressure.

Crucially, this step safeguards against one of the greatest threats to any human capital strategy: crisis hiring. When organizations are caught unprepared, they are more likely to make reactive decisions—sacrificing quality, cultural fit, and long-term potential to fill a role quickly. Forecast & Adjust acts as a defense mechanism, creating conditions that foster resilience and agility. It keeps the organization forward-looking and adaptable, even amid change.

GOVERNANCE OUTLINE

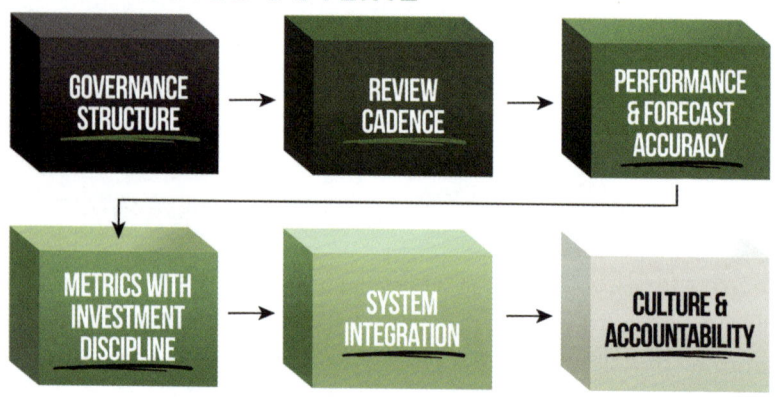

1. Governance Structure

- Establish a Human Capital Governance Council composed of HR, finance, strategy, and business unit executives.

- Assign specific roles to each member: HR leads talent planning and analytics; Finance reviews labor ROI; Strategy ensures alignment with long-range plans; Business Units provide operational forecasts and staffing needs.
- Ensure decision rights and escalation protocols are clearly defined.

2. Review Cadence

- Align governance routines with existing enterprise planning cycles, such as quarterly business reviews, annual budget cycles, and strategic refresh meetings.
- Schedule quarterly talent forecasting reviews and HCIS health checks, integrating real-time data from dashboards, business updates, and market intelligence.

3. Performance & Forecast Accuracy

- Implement a forecast-to-actuals process that compares workforce projections to real outcomes, including hiring timelines, turnover, promotion rates, and pipeline readiness.
- Use predictive accuracy scoring to assess how talent criteria aligns with outcomes and adjust models accordingly.

4. Metrics with Investment Discipline

- **Human Capital Efficiency Ratio:** Revenue per dollar spent on labor.
- **Return on Talent Investment:** Profit growth relative to talent spend.

- **Predictive Hiring Accuracy:** Percent of hires rated top performing after 12 months.
- **Internal Mobility Ratio:** Proportion of roles filled internally vs. externally.
- **Bench Strength Index:** Succession depth for critical roles.

5. System Integration

- Deploy integrated dashboards and analytics platforms for real-time visibility.
- Define talent risk triggers (e.g., leadership flight risk, pipeline vulnerability, skill shortages) that initiate proactive review.

6. Culture & Accountability

- Make talent outcomes a component of executive performance evaluations.
- Encourage talent stewardship by recognizing leaders who develop successors, improve internal mobility, and elevate team performance.
- Embed these principles into leadership competencies to create enterprise-wide alignment on the importance of forecasting and proactive talent management.

Governance ensures talent decisions are aligned to enterprise strategy, prevents reactive behavior, and reinforces investment discipline across the organization.

Governance transforms workforce planning from an operational task to a strategic advantage. It is the forum where data becomes decision and foresight becomes capability. Ultimately, forecasting and adjustment are what turn strategy into sustainability. It is not just about reviewing plans but about stewarding the HCP with the same rigor and foresight used in financial investments. In this continual cycle of observation, analysis, and realignment, the HCIS moves from theory to transformative value.

Artificial INTELLIGENCE

Artificial intelligence is not a mere accelerant to the Human Capital Investment Strategy—it is a force multiplier that challenges outdated thinking, expands strategic possibilities, and sharpens the imperative for disciplined, forward-looking investment in people.

At every phase of HCIS, AI transforms how organizations define, measure, and maximize the return on their human capital. It brings precision to planning, transparency to risk, and personalization to development. But it also demands a new level of discernment and governance to ensure that automation enhances rather than erodes the human aspects of work.

AI's value to HCIS begins with clarity. In Step One: Establish the Pro Forma, AI helps articulate a more rigorous investment thesis by linking workforce data directly to financial performance. Leaders can now quantify expected returns on workforce initiatives, benchmark against industry standards, and make more defensible decisions about where to invest. Platforms enable this financial rigor, positioning human capital not as an expense line, but as a lever for EBITDA growth.

From there, AI improves the fidelity of portfolio evaluation. In Step Two: Assess Portfolio, machine learning tools uncover hidden value within the organization. These platforms surface underleveraged high-potential talent, skill mismatches, and engagement gaps, often invisible through traditional means. This enables a more accurate picture of both current-state assets and latent capacity.

AI then deepens the risk lens. In Step Three: Stratify Risk, predictive analytics, like those offered by IBM WatsonX and PeopleAnalytics.io, detect succession vulnerabilities, flight risks, and key-person dependencies with over 90% accuracy. These tools use dynamic inputs—tenure, promotability, sentiment, and external labor demand—to proactively surface threats to workforce continuity before they manifest. Armed with that intelligence, leaders can act decisively.

In Step Four: Rebalance Allocations, AI facilitates real-time workforce optimization. Talent solutions can recommend redeployments, promotions, or transitions based on real-time business needs and evolving skills. Rather than static workforce planning, this is fluid resource allocation—putting the right people in the right place at the right time to generate outsized returns.

AI also expands the aperture of who gets considered. In Step Five: Expand Options, tools can apply AI to broaden candidate pools across dimensions of experience and background. By evaluating potential rather than pedigree, these platforms reduce bias and help build diverse, adaptable teams ready for an unpredictable future.

Which brings us to Step Six: Forecast and Adjust,

PERHAPS THE MOST CRITICAL ARENA WHERE AI SHIFTS THE PARADIGM.

In the past, workforce planning was a periodic exercise. But in an AI-integrated environment, forecasting becomes a continuous strategic function. Platforms can synthesize internal performance data with macroeconomic indicators, industry trends, and skill evolution to predict future talent needs. They can forecast skill obsolescence, emerging capability gaps, and potential internal mobility roadblocks—well before they impact business outcomes.

With this foresight, organizations can reinvest in targeted development through reskilling, upskilling, succession planning, or workforce redesign. AI does not just flag problems; it helps simulate solutions, model outcomes, and optimize talent pipelines. It enables leaders to shift from reactive talent replacement to proactive capacity building.

But this isn't without challenges. AI fundamentally disrupts traditional human capital assumptions. Job architectures must be reimagined as AI automates tasks previously considered human-only. Legacy performance metrics often fail to capture value in AI-augmented environments. Without governance, AI can amplify bias, turning a strategic asset into a reputational risk.

STILL, FOR ORGANIZATIONS WILLING TO EVOLVE, THE OPPORTUNITY IS IMMENSE.

AI allows human capital strategies to operate at the speed of business with unprecedented granularity. It enables personalization at scale—matching learning journeys to individual aspirations or detecting burnout before it leads to attrition. It repositions human work, elevating the uniquely human attributes of creativity, judgment, and collaboration, precisely because AI cannot replicate them.

In a world of increasingly commoditized technology, people become the competitive moat. The organizations that thrive will be those that treat human capital as an appreciating, adaptive asset—one that requires continual reinvestment, rigorous analysis, and strategic stewardship.

AI does not replace HCIS—it raises the stakes. It challenges our assumptions, accelerates our execution, and redefines the very nature of talent value. **Ultimately, however, it is not the algorithm that determines success. It is the investor behind it—the leader who chooses to invest not just in efficiency, but in potential.**

Conclusion

When human capital investment becomes an operationalized, data-driven process, organizations can pivot with agility, optimize talent, and sustain a competitive advantage in an ever-changing business landscape.

The shift to human capital as a competitive advantage is not merely theoretical but an operational imperative. Organizations that successfully integrate HCIS into their daily operations will build resilient, high-performing, and future-ready workforces, ensuring long-term success in an ever-evolving business landscape.

To fully operationalize HCIS, organizations must go beyond individual steps and create a culture of investment-thinking at all levels. Senior executives must champion HCIS as a strategic priority and ensure it is integrated into business planning.

Senior leaders must embrace human capital as a strategic investment that directly impacts competitive advantage, innovation, and long-term business sustainability. This mindset shift requires more than policy updates or structural adjustments; it demands a fundamental transformation in how organizations perceive, develop, and deploy their talent. HCIS is not simply an HR initiative; it is a core business strategy that must be embedded in decision-making at every level.

However, embedding this philosophy into an organization's DNA requires more than intent—it requires execution. Moving from theory to practice means navigating resistance, shifting mindsets, and reinforcing behaviors that support a culture of continuous investment in people. This is where change management becomes critical.

Part Two of this book focuses on the cultural transformation necessary to sustain HCIS over the long term.

Even the best investment frameworks will falter without a deliberate, well-structured change management strategy. True success lies not only in creating a human capital strategy but in enabling a culture that embraces it—one where investing in people is as natural and expected as investing in technology, innovation, and infrastructure.

IMPLEMENTING
STEP SIX

I. OVERVIEW & OBJECTIVES
- **Objective**

  Build a continuous, intelligence-driven system that monitors internal workforce dynamics, anticipates future talent needs, and adjusts investments in real time based on evolving conditions.

- **Key Message**

- Human capital is not a static asset. Like any dynamic portfolio, it must be actively monitored and adjusted. Forecasting is how you anticipate inflection points. Adjustment is how you stay agile under pressure.

- **Mindset Shif**

- Treat talent forecasting like financial modeling: grounded in data, revisited frequently, and stress-tested under multiple scenarios.

II. STEP-BY-STEP ACTION PLAN

1. Establish a Talent Forecasting Framework

- **Purpose**

- Create an executive-level forecasting model that links business projections with workforce capacity and capability.

- **Actions**
  - **Set a Forecasting Cadence:** Conduct monthly or quarterly reviews across HR, finance, strategy, and business unit executives.

  - **Build Cross-Functional Teams:** Involve leaders from sales, operations, strategy, finance, and HR.

  - **Use Scenario Planning:** Model best-, base-, and worst-case business scenarios and their talent implications.

- **Key Message**
  Anticipation creates advantage. Don't let your workforce plan lag behind your business plan.

2. Define and Track Core Workforce Metrics

- **Purpose**
  Identify the indicators that signal when, where, and how to adjust human capital strategy.

- **Key Metrics to Monitor**
  - Attrition (voluntary/involuntary/regrettable)
  - Internal mobility rates
  - Open roles vs. target headcount
  - Time-to-fill for critical positions
  - Promotion velocity
  - Learning completion rates

— Forecasted vs. actual talent demand

- **Actions**
  - Integrate these metrics into board and operational reviews.
  - Build automated alerts for key thresholds (e.g., "ready-now" bench drops below 1x coverage).

- **Pro Tip**
  Make workforce data as visible and real time as financial data.

3. Align Talent Forecasts with Strategic Business Planning

- **Purpose**
  Ensure talent investment decisions are directly informed by growth, transformation, or cost containment initiatives.

- **Actions**
  - Overlay workforce forecasts on strategic plans:
    o New market entries
    o Product expansions
    o Digital transformation efforts
    o M&A activity
  - Factor in lead times for:
    o Sourcing and onboarding
    o Development for critical roles

o   Knowledge transfer and succession readiness

- **Key Message**
  Talent should never be an afterthought in strategy. It's the execution engine.

4. Implement Governance and Adjustment Protocols

- **Purpose**
  Build executive discipline around forecasting accountability and adjustment actions.

- **Actions**
  — **Establish Governance Policies:** Define who owns each part of the forecast and who authorizes adjustments.

  — **Create Forecast vs. Actual Reports:** Review past assumptions, accuracy, and deviations.

  — **Document Lessons Learned:** Treat misses as strategic data, not personal failure.

- **Pro Tip**
  Forecasting is never perfect. Adjustment is the mark of maturity, not failure.

5. Build a Culture of Agility and Continuous Reallocation

- **Purpose**
  Embed forecasting into the operating rhythm of

leadership, HR, and strategy.

- **Actions**

  - **Educate Leaders:** Train on how to read, interpret, and act on forecasting data.

  - **Normalize Mid-Cycle Adjustments:** Shift development resources, hiring targets, or internal mobility priorities based on updated forecasts.

  - **Reward Foresight:** Recognize leaders who anticipate future needs and act early.

- **Key Message**

  Being wrong isn't the problem—being rigid is. The best leaders course-correct faster than the market.

6. Operationalize Talent Portfolio Reviews

- **Purpose**

  Make talent evaluation an ongoing executive function, not an annual HR exercise.

- **Actions**

  - Schedule quarterly or biannual portfolio reviews as part of business reviews.

  - Review individual movement between quadrants over time (talent velocity).

  - Integrate reviews with succession planning, internal mobility, and promotion decisions.

- **Checklist for Talent Reviews**

  - Are we developing or stalling our high potentials?

- — Are our top performers engaged and retained?
- — Are we tolerating underperformance due to lack of visibility or courage?
- — Are we over-relying on a narrow bench of "go-to" people?
- **Pro Tip**
  Just as investors track portfolio performance quarterly, talent portfolios should be revisited regularly for rebalancing.

7. Digitize Human Capital Evaluation

- **Purpose**
  Build a digital, integrated approach to managing and analyzing workforce performance at scale.
- **Actions**
  - — Develop dashboards with real-time visibility into key indicators:
    - o Talent density by function
    - o Risk-adjusted succession coverage
    - o Promotion and development velocity
    - o Demographic and cognitive diversity... distribution
  - — Link these dashboards to strategic metrics (e.g., revenue per FTE, engagement-to-retention correlation).
  - — Automate alerts for emerging risks (e.g., top performer disengagement, succession gaps).

- **Key Message**
  Real-time talent intelligence enables agile work-force decisions—faster, more innovative, and more aligned with market realities.

III. TOOLS
www.cynthiabentzenmercer.com/resources

- Human Capital Investment Strategy Framework
- HCIS Governance Outline

IV. NEXT STEP
With a real-time, responsive investment system now in place, integrate all six HCIS steps into an annual Human Capital Review Cycle—formalizing the connection between people decisions and enterprise value creation.

PART ONE

Conclusion

EXECUTIVE SUMMARY

The six steps of the HCIS are not theoretical ideals—they are a disciplined, actionable model for converting your workforce into a durable competitive advantage. Together, they reframe human capital as a strategic asset class, demanding the same rigor, analysis, and intentionality you apply to your financial portfolio.

Here is a recap of each step—and how to begin putting it to work.

 Step One: Establish Pro Forma
Articulate your investment thesis: Define what return you expect from your human capital, quantified in terms of growth, innovation, quality, retention, customer experience, or market position. This becomes your strategic North Star. Without it, you are managing labor as a cost center, not investing in it as an appreciating asset.

Next move: Align your executive team on how talent drives enterprise value.

 Step Two: Assess Portfolio
Map the current allocation of talent: Where is your talent currently placed? Where is it over-performing,

under-leveraged, or hidden? Conduct a full audit of roles, capabilities, and outcomes to assess your existing portfolio's strength and balance.

Next move: Segment your workforce by strategic value, not just organizational charts or levels.

 ### Step Three: **Stratify Risk**
Quantify exposure to human capital–related threats: Identify vulnerabilities such as succession gaps, turnover sensitivity, key-person dependency, or lack of skill depth. Human capital risk is not theoretical; it is quantifiable, measurable, and predictive.

Next move: Introduce a Talent Risk Index and assess your most exposed roles.

 ### Step Four: **Rebalance Allocations**
Shift resources where they generate the most significant return: Disrupt default allocation models. Prioritize high-leverage, high-potential roles for investment. Reduce resource drag where performance or strategic alignment is weak. This is where talent strategy becomes capital strategy.

Next move: Build an investment case for reallocating development, compensation, or leadership attention.

 ### Step Five: **Expand Options**
Diversify your talent strategy: Just as a financial portfolio requires diversification for resilience, so does your human capital. Broaden cognitive, experiential, and demographic representation. Expand access to opportunity. Rethink pipelines, not just roles.

Next move: Identify where referral bias or sameness is shrinking your future optionality.

 Step Six: Forecast and Adjust
Look ahead—and course-correct in real time: Use scenario planning, workforce analytics, and market trends to anticipate what is next. Strategic workforce planning is not a static spreadsheet. It is a living, breathing part of capital governance.

Next move: Establish a quarterly cadence of forecasting and rebalancing human capital investments.

· ·

FROM INSIGHT TO *Intentionality*

These six steps are not a one-time initiative. They form a cycle of investment, evaluation, and reinvestment. When used consistently, the HCIS framework unlocks compounding returns—not just in performance, but in trust, innovation, retention, and leadership continuity.

THE MOST IMPORTANT NEXT STEP IS NOT PERFECT EXECUTION. IT IS STRATEGIC COMMITMENT AND CULTURAL ENABLEMENT.

Part Two provides the tools to build the cultural infrastructure that sustains HCIS. We'll explore the change management practices, leadership behaviors, and governance mechanisms that turn strategy into shared belief and belief into sustained performance. Even the most sophisticated investment strategy will stall without a culture ready to receive, reinforce, and accelerate it.

Let's begin the work of turning insight into institutional habit.

PART TWO

ENABLING A
Human CAPITAL
INVESTMENT CULTURE

PART TWO

ORGANIZATIONAL CHANGE

FROM EFFECTING (N.) TO AFFECTING (V.) CHANGE

Wells Fargo, one of the largest banks in the United States, faced one of the most publicized failures of organizational culture in modern corporate history. The bank was long recognized for its aggressive, sales-driven culture, where employees felt pressure to meet stringent cross-selling targets. However, when leadership attempted to shift the company's culture towards ethical banking practices following a massive fraud scandal, the effort failed due to inadequate change management.

For years, Wells Fargo operated under an aggressive "eight is great" sales strategy, in which employees were pressured to sell at least eight products per customer. This high-pressure environment resulted in widespread unethical behavior, including the unauthorized opening of millions of accounts. In 2016, the scandal came to light, leading to $185 million in fines, the resignation of key executives, and significant reputational damage for Wells Fargo.

Following the scandal, the company undertook a comprehensive cultural transformation, shifting from a sales-driven environment to one centered on ethics, transparency, and customer trust. The new leadership team emphasized integrity and compliance, restructured incentive programs, and introduced new risk management measures. While ethically well intended, **this effort largely failed to gain traction due to inadequate change management.**

Where Change Management Failed:

1. Failure to Address Deeply Rooted Norms
Middle managers, who had been promoted based on sales performance, struggled to adopt the new customer-centric approach.

2. Lack of Employee Buy-In
Employees were instructed to abandon old practices but were not provided with clear guidance on the expected behaviors, other than simply avoiding unethical practices.

3. Inconsistent Leadership Messaging
Senior executives promoted cultural change, but many middle managers continued to measure success based on sales performance, sending mixed signals to employees.

4. Failure to Implement a Phased Approach
Instead of gradually shifting away from sales quotas while reinforcing new behaviors, the bank attempted a rapid pivot without proper reskilling or adaptation periods.

5. Ignoring Employee Feedback & Resistance
Some teams found workarounds to continue meeting old performance standards, undermining the cultural shift.

By 2020, Wells Fargo was still struggling to repair its culture, facing new scandals and regulatory scrutiny. Despite leadership changes and renewed efforts, the bank remained a cautionary tale of how failed organizational transformation can undermine trust, performance, and long-term viability.

While the shift to HCIS does not intend to correct unethical or unlawful behavior, it requires the same level of strategic foresight and disciplined execution as any large-scale cultural change.

The lessons from Wells Fargo's missteps highlight a crucial truth:

No matter how well designeda strategy may be, its success ultimately relies on the human element—

HOW PEOPLE PERCEIVE, ADOPT, AND SUSTAIN THE CHANGE.

At this point, the six steps of HCIS have been fully outlined, supported by empirical evidence, and presented with clear implementation guidelines. However, just as financial investing requires a sound strategy and the proper behavioral discipline to generate returns, investing in human capital demands not only a framework but also a culture that supports it. **Before implementing Steps Two through Six, organizations must first establish a change management strategy**—one that aligns leadership, engages employees, and ensures that the transition to an investment-driven culture is sustainable and impactful.

One approach to scaling HCIS and its accompanying change management strategy is to start with the top two to three layers of leadership. This allows time to develop the infrastructure and talent literacy while also demonstrating to employees that leadership is held to the same standards. Companies that implement an investment culture from the top-down gain trust and build confidence.

THE COST OF *Failed* CHANGE MANAGEMENT

Transitioning from viewing labor as an expense burden to seeing it as an investment in human capital is not merely a structural shift, but a paradigm shift. Research by McKinsey & Company indicates that organizations with robust change management initiatives are 3.5 times more likely to outperform their industry peers. However, Kotter International and Prosci studies show that approximately **70% of all change management efforts fail**. These failures are often attributed to a lack of executive sponsorship, resistance due to perceived loss, change fatigue, unintended consequences, and insufficient reinforcement mechanisms.

Using the Wells Fargo framework of failed change management, consider the following potential missteps of an HCIS transformation:

1. **Failure to Address Deeply Rooted Norms**
   Middle managers, who have hired employees based on likability and years of experience, struggle to adopt the new talent mindset.

2. **Lack of Employee Buy-In**
   Leaders are instructed to abandon old practices but are not provided with education on the expected behaviors, other than being encouraged to focus on the candidate's natural talent.

3. **Inconsistent Leadership Messaging**
   Senior executives promote cultural change, but many middle managers still measure success based on filling

open positions as quickly as possible, sending mixed signals to employees.

4. Failure to Implement a Phased Approach
Instead of taking the time to introduce, educate, and redesign the HCIS processes, the organization mandates a rapid pivot without proper reskilling or adaptation periods.

5. Ignoring Employee Feedback & Resistance
Without reinforcement strategies in place, teams find workarounds to continue meeting old performance standards, undermining the cultural shift.

Failure to manage change effectively results in quantifiable costs. The *Harvard Business Review* reports that **unsuccessful change initiatives result in an average annual productivity loss of 5%–10%,** as employees experience confusion, disengagement, or outright opposition. Responses to change can be significant disruptors, and their impact should not be underestimated.

··

CONSIDER *Stakeholders*

One of the most critical elements of successful change management is accurately identifying every individual with whom the shift will directly or indirectly impact. Implementing HCIS introduces significant change, beginning with the HR function and closely followed by hiring leaders.

Despite mounting evidence supporting the use of validated tools, evidence-based assessments remain underutilized. Many HR practitioners and leaders are either unaware of the research or skeptical of its relevance. Building literacy around the predictive validity of selection methods is essential, but doing so also challenges long-held habits and traditions that many professionals have relied upon for years.

For some, assessments are perceived as a threat to professional autonomy. HR leaders who take pride in their ability to "read people" may feel that using formal instruments diminishes their judgment, experience, or the credit they receive for hiring decisions. This can create resistance, even when the data strongly supports improved outcomes.

Moreover, there is a widespread belief that more information naturally leads to better decisions. However, research indicates that adding irrelevant or invalid data to valid assessments often reduces predictive accuracy, even as it increases confidence in subjective, holistic judgments (Dana et al., 2013; Kausel et al., 2016). In other words, more data does not always mean better decisions, especially when that data muddles the signal.

··

REACTIONS TO *Change*

Recognizing the significant transformation that HCIS can bring to an organization, as well as the natural discomfort it may cause, a comprehensive change management strategy is essential. Without proactive management, employees will respond based on the information they possess, or worse, their misconceptions. This is particularly crucial for leaders, as they will evaluate change through two key questions:

1. *How does this change impact the company or my employees?*
2. *How does this change impact me?*

Depending on the effectiveness of the change management strategy, leaders' responses to change generally fall into four main categories.

Reactions to Change

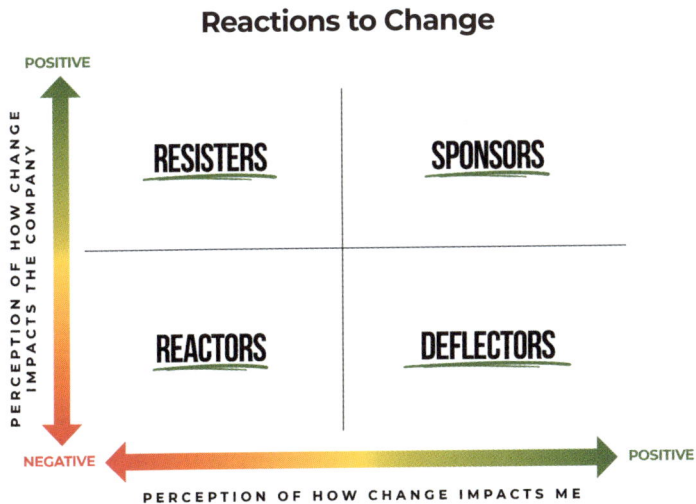

A reactor views the change as a net negative for both the organization and themselves. This mindset stems from loss aversion, a well-documented behavioral bias in which people tend to fear losses more than they appreciate equivalent gains. For instance, a reactor might worry that adopting predictive talent science will expose and threaten employees who have been protected or that it could challenge their competencies. This shift can feel personally and professionally threatening without a clear understanding of strength management and the organization's intentions.

REACTOR

A reactor views the change as a net negative for both the organization and themselves. This mindset stems from loss aversion, a well-documented behavioral bias in which people tend to fear losses more than they appreciate equivalent gains. For instance, a reactor might worry that adopting predictive talent science will expose and threaten employees who have been protected or that it could challenge their competencies. This shift can feel personally and professionally threatening without a clear understanding of strength management and the organization's intentions.

RESISTER

A resister may intellectually understand how HCIS benefits the organization but may still resist due to self-interest. A common concern is that identifying poor performers could lead to forced terminations, leaving the organization short-staffed in a competitive labor market. This reaction aligns with findings from the *Journal of Organizational Behavior*, which states that employees who feel threatened by change are 60% more likely to disengage or undermine the initiative.

DEFLECTOR

A deflector recognizes the personal benefits of HCIS but grapples with the perceived effects on others. High-performing individuals in leadership positions often face a psychological phenomenon known as "moral distress," where they experience guilt over actions that adversely affect their peers. Rather than promoting change, a deflector may shift blame onto the company, positioning themselves as a passive or even covert opponent to HCIS adoption.

SPONSOR

The desired reaction is sponsorship. These leaders view HCIS as a strategic advantage that benefits both the organization and themselves. Sponsors are not only open to change but also actively promote it. Research by Prosci indicates that strong executive sponsorship increases the likelihood of success for change initiatives by 72%. Sponsors are most effective when they have a clear understanding of HCIS.

CHANGE
MANAGEMENT

To cultivate a network of sponsors, change management should be implemented through three core components: Align, Affect, and Assess. The process should begin with the CEO and executive leadership, cascading downward in all cases.

CHANGE MANAGEMENT *Strategy*

Change Management Strategy

- **Define Change**
- **Evaluate Readiness**
- **Create a Change Management Plan**

- **Develop Champions**
- **Build Readiness**

- **Evaluate Impact**
- **Standardize to Scale**
- **Reinforce Change**

Align

Affect

Assess

ALIGN

The first phase, *align*, sets the foundation for successful implementation by securing organizational buy-in through three essential actions: defining the change, evaluating readiness, and developing a robust change management plan. According to Prosci's research on change initiatives, projects with excellent change management are six times more likely to meet or exceed objectives than those with poor change management practices. Alignment is not simply about agreement; it is about clarity, coherence, and commitment.

1. Define Change

Though seemingly straightforward, defining the change is a common stumbling block. Leaders must have unwavering clarity on why the change is necessary, what outcomes it aims to drive, and how it will impact both the organization and individuals at every level.

In the context of the HCIS, the change should be framed not as a mere HR initiative but as a business transformation—an imperative driven by market forces, talent scarcity, and the need for agility. The goal is to leverage predictive analytics to optimize selection and development decisions, align talent with business priorities, and build a sustainable competitive advantage. This articulation must go beyond vision statements to include use cases, anticipated challenges, and expected returns on investment. Change that is not well defined becomes difficult to defend, promote, or implement.

2. Evaluate Readiness

Step Three of the HCIS framework, Stratify Risk, emphasizes the importance of understanding and mitigating leadership risk tolerance. Research by the Corporate

Executive Board (now part of Gartner) found that organizations conducting formal readiness assessments experience 40% less resistance and 30% faster implementation.

A practical readiness evaluation comprises three key components: 1) the degree of shared understanding across stakeholder groups, 2) the existence and strength of the infrastructure required to support HCIS (including technology, systems, and policies), and 3) the availability of resources—human, financial, and temporal. Additionally, a cultural audit can identify whether the organizational climate is conducive to the shift in mindset required by HCIS. Resistance often stems not from the change itself, but from fear, ambiguity, or a lack of capacity to adapt.

3. Develop a Change Management Plan

Once alignment is achieved and readiness confirmed, a structured change management plan must be developed. This plan should reflect the diverse needs of stakeholders, including frontline managers, HR teams, executives, and employees. The change model highlights the importance of creating a sense of urgency, building coalitions, and institutionalizing new steps that must be embedded into the HCIS implementation road map.

The plan must be both strategic and tactical, incorporating communication schedules, feedback loops, reinforcement mechanisms, and defined responsibilities. Equally important is preparing for emotional responses to change, such as grief, fear, excitement, and skepticism, and equipping leaders to manage these emotions with empathy and transparency.

AFFECT

Change is not enacted through plans alone—it must be internalized and activated at every level. The *affect* phase focuses on cultivating psychological and behavioral readiness by developing champions and building readiness.

1. Develop Champions

Early adopters function as internal influencers. They play a critical role in accelerating adoption by demonstrating new behaviors, building peer credibility, and acting as cultural multipliers. Drawing on Everett Rogers's Diffusion of Innovations theory, the successful diffusion of any innovation requires reaching a critical mass of approximately 16% adoption—the "tipping point" that propels the system toward sustained transformation.

These champions should be intentionally selected across functions and levels to mirror the diversity of the organization. According to research from the Center for Creative Leadership, peers are often the most trusted source of change information. Training champions to actively listen, address concerns, and share wins publicly transforms them into credible agents of change, rather than mouthpieces of leadership.

2. Build Readiness

One of the most significant obstacles to HCIS adoption is the myth of universal coachability—that anyone can become excellent in any role with the proper development. While well intentioned, this mindset dilutes the strategic intent of talent optimization. HCIS requires a foundational shift in how organizations understand human potential—not as limitless, but as unique and directional.

Readiness, therefore, includes leadership development in talent literacy, behavioral prediction, and data-driven selection. According to Deloitte's *Global Human Capital Trends Report*, only 17% of companies believe they possess the tools and skills to effectively utilize talent data. HCIS demands that leaders become literate in the science of potential, not just instinct or experience, and view hiring and development decisions as long-term capital investments, rather than short-term staffing transactions.

ASSESS

The third and final phase, *assess*, ensures that change becomes embedded in the organization's culture and operations. This phase comprises evaluating the impact, standardizing to scale, and reinforcing for sustainability.

1. Evaluate Impact

As HCIS takes root, organizations should expect a different profile of workforce dynamics. Due to stricter predictive modeling, fewer candidates may progress to final interviews, and this intentional selectivity may initially frustrate hiring managers. However, research from the *Harvard Business Review* shows that high-performing organizations prioritize fit over speed, understanding that a single high-potential hire delivers returns that far exceed the cost of vacancies.

Organizations may also experience natural attrition from individuals who are misaligned with the new culture or expectations. While this can cause short-term disruption, it often signals positive recalibration. A 2022 study by Gallup showed that organizations that proactively manage employee fit and potential experience 21% higher profitability. This phase's assessment must be quantitative (turnover rates, performance metrics, and quality of hire) and qualitative (manager feedback, candidate experience, and cultural alignment).

2. Standardize to Scale

Scaling HCIS across the organization requires more than duplicating processes—it demands consistent application of principles. Begin with executive and mission-critical roles, where the stakes and impact are most visible. As the infrastructure stabilizes and lessons emerge, gradually expand to other areas.

Scalability depends on automation, repeatable systems, and strong governance. According to Bersin by Deloitte, companies with mature talent strategies are twice as likely to outperform peers in revenue per employee. Standardizing predictive models, decision criteria, and feedback protocols ensures that HCIS remains disciplined even as it grows.

3. Reinforce the Change

A primary reason change efforts falter is the absence of reinforcement. Old behaviors tend to reemerge when exceptions are made or leaders are not held accountable. A study published in the *Journal of Change Management* found that reinforcement was the single most predictive factor of long-term success in change.

Reinforcement must be proactive and public: celebrating quick wins, spotlighting success stories, and instituting consequences for noncompliance. Accountability structures, such as executive sponsorship, dashboard reporting, and embedded KPIs, convey that this change is not optional.

Leading
ORGANIZATIONAL CHANGE

True and lasting transformation requires every leader, decision-maker, and influential person within the organization to deliver a consistent message, model expected behaviors, and measure success with tangible outcomes.

Without reinforcement, even the best change initiatives fade into irrelevance, replaced by the comfort of old habits.

In my experience leading large-scale changes, those that failed or were not sustained were ultimately tied to a lack of executive leadership, as illustrated in the following example: the implementation of HCIS in a large organization. At the onset, every step was meticulously executed, and a solid change management plan was in place. The COO was a key sponsor and champion, which was critical as the change impacted all of his direct reports. Over a five-year period, messaging, modeling, and measurement were consistently demonstrated by executive leadership, and the HCIS became embedded in the fabric of the organization.

Upon the retirement of the COO, the intentional execution of HCIS began to wane. Within two years of the COO's departure, the organization reverted to traditional selection practices, prioritizing speed over predictive validity. The staffing shortage that followed the pandemic exacerbated the inclination to revert to what felt familiar and safe. The result was continued financial challenges, panic staffing during the busy season, followed by annual layoffs prior to the end of the fiscal year.

MESSAGE

Change begins with communication, but it is sustained through consistent messaging at every level. When leaders reinforce the vision, articulate the rationale behind the change, and align every decision with the desired outcome, they build credibility.

The message must be clear, compelling, and repeated often. People need to hear it multiple times before it becomes ingrained in their minds. It should be tied to both logic and emotion—why this change matters and what it means for employees, customers, and the organization's future.

MODEL

People tend to believe what they see more than what they hear. Leaders cannot just talk about change; they must embody it. Employees look to leadership to determine whether new expectations are real or just another corporate initiative destined to fade.

Leaders must demonstrate change in their daily actions, reinforcing new behaviors in decision-making, employee interactions, and navigating challenges.

If leaders deviate from the change, employees will follow suit. The fastest way to kill momentum is for leaders to operate by different rules.

MEASURE

Change becomes real when it is measurable. Without clear, quantifiable expectations, new behaviors remain optional rather than required. Success must be tracked, analyzed, and reported. What gets measured gets managed.

Leaders must connect performance metrics to change, reinforcing new standards, not old benchmarks to define success.

Recognition plays a critical role, celebrating those who embrace the new way and calling out those who resist it.

Organizations that fail in this stage, where influential leaders are not held accountable, allow exceptions that become the norm. Employees notice and assume the change is not required.

THE *Power* OF LEADERSHIP

Change is not an event; it is a sustained effort. Message, Model, and Measure ensure that transformation does not remain a temporary initiative but becomes ingrained in the organization's DNA. When leaders convey a consistent message, employees are more likely to understand and believe in the change. When leaders exhibit expected behavior, employees tend to follow. When leaders assess success and enforce accountability, change becomes reality.

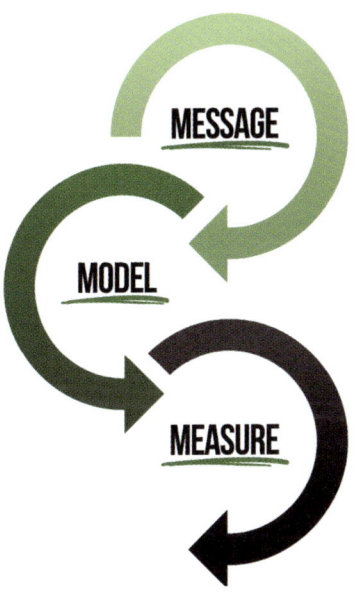

Every leader, at every level, plays a role in sustaining change. **The question is not whether people will follow—it is whether leadership is committed enough to ensure they do.**

CASE STUDY:

Centers for Disease Control and Prevention (CDC)

Enabling an Investment Culture at the CDC

In the early 2000s, the U.S. Centers for Disease Control and Prevention (CDC) embarked on a high-stakes effort to modernize its pediatric vaccine distribution network. The existing system was inefficient, costly, and fragmented—over 400 independent vaccine depots across the U.S. operated with little integration, transparency, or real-time delivery capabilities.

To help lead this transformation, the CDC recruited Reginald Mebane, a former Chief Operating Officer at FedEx Trade Networks, into the Senior Executive Service (SES)—the top leadership tier of the U.S. federal government. Mebane's appointment reflected a bold choice: Rather than hire from within traditional public health channels, the CDC chose a private-sector executive known for operational excellence and supply chain modernization.

What followed was not only a model of operational innovation but also an extraordinary exercise in cultural transformation, aligned to each step of the HCIS framework.

- **Organizational Change:**
  When Reginald Mebane was recruited to the CDC to help modernize its vaccine supply chain, he entered a deeply complex, heavily regulated

environment. The organization had more than 400 separate vaccine depots, lacked end-to-end visibility, and was burdened by contractual inefficiencies. While the logistical issues were formidable, the greater challenge lay in navigating the cultural, structural, and human capital barriers to change.

- **The Cost of Failed Change Management:**
  The risk of failure was significant. Resistance from internal stakeholders, state health departments, and political leaders created a fragile foundation for success. Without careful attention to culture and change dynamics, the CDC could have experienced deeper inefficiencies, morale decline, and public trust erosion. Instead, Mebane executed a strategy that embedded change into both operational and human capital systems.

- **Consider Stakeholders:**
  The stakeholder map was expansive: internal employees protected by union agreements and merit-based employment systems; agency leaders with legacy expectations; state partners facing the loss of contracts; and political actors with visibility into federal funding streams. Mebane understood that his strategy required not just process change, but stakeholder navigation.

- **Reactions to Change:**
Mebane encountered the full spectrum of change reactions:

  - **Reactors** who feared losing legacy contracts and local control
  - **Resisters** who opposed external leadership and operational modernization
  - **Deflectors** who appeared to agree but quietly undermined momentum
  - **Sponsors**, including the CDC Director and Chief Operating Officer, who supported bold changes but needed proof of sustained value

Change Management Strategy

To advance a human capital investment mindset and implement large-scale systems transformation, Mebane applied a deliberate change management model, emphasizing communication, transparency, and top-down alignment.

- **Align:**
Mebane built strong partnerships with the top of the house. He partnered with senior leaders, such as Dr. Mitch Cohen, to jointly deliver tough messages and build credibility across business and scientific units. He aligned the modernization effort with broader CDC goals, including fiscal responsibility, operational excellence, and public health equity.

- **Affect:**
  Cultural legacy was a significant barrier. Before launching any major changes, Mebane commissioned a "Cultural DNA" study to conduct a comprehensive assessment of the organization. This surfaced passive-aggressive communication norms, fear of external leaders, and "appearance of consensus" behavior that masked dissent. Rather than charging forward blindly, he used this insight to tailor his communication, adapt pacing, and build early champions.

- **Assess:**
  Understanding the impact required Mebane to identify everyone affected by the changes, from administrative assistants to state-level logistics partners. He conducted town halls, skip-level meetings, and one-on-one engagements to map concerns, gather input, and demonstrate transparency. By identifying both pain points and hidden allies, he created a responsive engagement plan.

Leading Organizational Change

- **Message:**
  Mebane crafted a clear and compelling narrative: Real-time vaccine delivery would save money, improve outcomes, and align the CDC with 21st-century capabilities. But he also humanized the message, acknowledging fear and honoring legacy contributions.

- **Model:**
  He modeled the behaviors he expected of others. He showed up personally at meetings, built relationships across silos, and took ownership of tough decisions. His actions reflected the very accountability and integrity he was asking others to demonstrate.

- **Measure:**
  The transformation yielded measurable results, as the McKesson contract consolidated 400 depots into three strategic centers, delivering vaccines with FedEx-like precision. Operational savings were substantial, though politically sensitive. More importantly, the system remains in place today, nearly two decades later.

- **The Power of Leadership:**
  Mebane's leadership was grounded in emotional and social intelligence and profound change acumen. With a background as a psychotherapist and a student of human behavior, he anticipated resistance and focused on influence over authority. His belief: "If I can't move the system, I will move people through relationships, clarity, and trust."

Organizational Readiness

Unlike the private sector, the federal government does not always move at the speed of business. Leaders cannot reassign staff easily or restructure teams at will. But readiness can be cultivated. By combining strategic alignment, internal advocacy, and adaptive communication, Mebane created the conditions necessary for lasting transformation.

Conclusion

This case exemplifies how an investment culture can be enabled even in the most complex systems. Through thoughtful stakeholder management, change leadership, and a human capital lens, the CDC's vaccine logistics operations transitioned from a state of fragmentation to one of fluency. The system Mebane helped design has endured precisely because it treated human capital as the linchpin of success.

His story is a powerful reminder that investment cultures are not installed by mandate—they are enabled by leaders who respect the power of people, understand the complexity of systems, and communicate a vision worth following.

ORGANIZATIONAL READINESS

Readiness is not a one-time checkpoint;

IT IS A RECURRING ASSESSMENT THAT GUIDES WHETHER AND HOW TO PROCEED.

After the *align* and *affect* phases, a formal reassessment should be conducted. Organizations with strong alignment and demonstrated effective engagement are significantly more likely to succeed in fully realizing HCIS.

Without alignment, implementation will be met with passive resistance or active sabotage. Without readiness, leaders may feel unsupported and unprepared, resulting in inconsistent application and ultimately leading to the abandonment of the strategy. Change is only sustainable when both the will and the way exist in tandem.

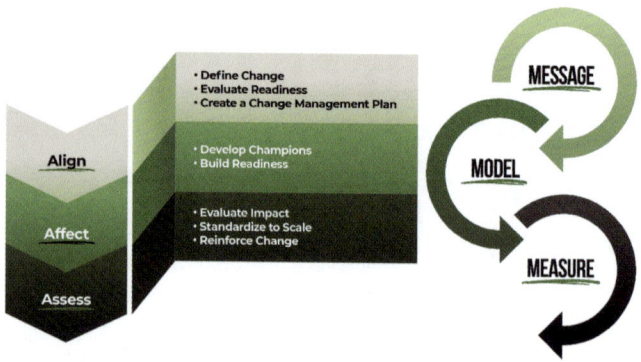

Change Management Model Leading Change

Conclusion

The HCIS framework empowers organizations to outperform the market by treating talent as a high-value, appreciating asset rather than a fixed cost. However, its success is not determined solely by policy changes; it relies on leaders' ability to drive and sustain meaningful change. This is not a one-time HR initiative or a tactical workforce adjustment; it is a strategic, enterprise-wide transformation that demands vision, discipline, and unwavering commitment from executives.

Without a deliberate and structured change management strategy, even the most well-designed HCIS will struggle to take root. Organizations must move beyond reactive decision-making and embrace a proactive approach—one that continuously aligns human capital investments with long-term business objectives. When leaders effectively manage this transition, they do not just respond to market shifts; they shape them, securing a sustainable competitive advantage that positions their organization for enduring success.

IMPLEMENTING AN INVESTMENT CULTURE

ORGANIZATIONAL READINESS *Assessment*

- Strongly Agree: 4
- Agree: 3
- Disagree: 2
- Strongly Disagree: 1

Section 1: Leadership & Strategic Commitment.

1. Our CEO and executive leadership actively champion human capital investment as a core business strategy.

2. Human capital investment is operationally informed and integrated across all business functions, rather than being siloed within H3.

3. Our leaders recognize that human capital investment is a strategic lever for enhancing financial performance, not merely a cost to manage.

4. Leaders across the organization are engaged in

developing talent and do not relegate this effort solely to HR or recruitment.

Section 2: Leadership Competency in Talent Assessment

1. Leaders in our organization are competent at objectively assessing employee performance.

2. Leaders are competent at evaluating employee talent fit for the current role.

3. Leaders are confident in identifying poor performers who are miscast and need repositioning.

4. Leaders can distinguish between employees who are poor performers with strong potential and those who are fundamentally misaligned with the role.

5. Leaders understand that not all employees can be developed to excellence in every role and are willing to make necessary role adjustments.

Section 3: Risk, Justice, & Talent Optimization.

1. Our organization takes an objective, data-driven approach to assessing and stratifying human capital risky.

2. Leaders are comfortable identifying organizational vulnerabilities related to talent gaps, skills shortages, and workforce planning.

3. Our leadership team strikes a balance between fairness and justice, recognizing that equal resource allocation may not always be the most effective or strategic approach to talent development.

4. Leaders are comfortable making differentiated investments in high-impact talent, even when it challenges traditional notions of fairness.

Section 4: Broadening Sourcing & Talent Strateg1.

1. Our talent acquisition strategy encompasses non-traditional sources, including career switchers, self-taught professionals, gig workers, and individuals returning to the workforce.

2. We actively challenge traditional hiring criteria (e.g., degrees, years of experience) to focus on competencies and potential.

3. We leverage validated talent assessments and alternative evaluation methods to identify untapped talent.

4. Our organization ensures that talent acquisition is fully aligned with long-term human capital investment strategies, rather than a short-term hiring function.

Section 5: Financial Alignment & ROI on Human Capital Investment

1. Human capital investment is integrated into financial strategy rather than being treated as a separate HR function.

2. We track and measure the financial impact of human capital investments, including productivity, retention, and innovation.

3. Leaders do not perceive human capital investment as time-consuming or disruptive but rather as an essential driver of business success.

4. Our organization is open to re-evaluating compensation structures to better align with motivation, performance, and long-term talent retention.

Section 6: Readiness for Change & Implementation

1. Our organization has a track record of successfully implementing strategic change initiatives.

2. Key stakeholders (CEO, HR, Finance, Operations) collaborate effectively on workforce planning and investment.

3. Our leadership team has access to relevant data and insights to drive human capital investment decisions.

4. Leaders are prepared to make hard decisions about talent, even when it challenges traditional structures or norms.

SCORING & INTERPRETATION

High Readiness (92 – 100):

Your organization is ready for immediate action. With strong alignment across leadership, cultural readiness, and operational capacity, you are well positioned to develop and implement a Human Capital Investment Strategy (HCIS). Utilize the complete set of tools and frameworks in HCIS to speed up execution, and apply integrated change management principles to ensure long-term adoption and impact.

Moderate Readiness (80 – 91):

Your organization has essential building blocks in place but may lack consistency in leadership alignment, risk visibility, or financial integration. Utilize the HCIS framework to reinforce these areas and adopt a disciplined, step-by-step approach. Change management principles will be crucial to enhance engagement, secure cross-functional buy-in, and embed the strategy into daily operations.

Low Readiness (<80):

Your organization may need to first establish leadership commitment, build internal capability, and connect human capital priorities to financial outcomes. Before proceeding, revisit each step of the HCIS framework with intentionality. Focus on fostering shared understanding, securing executive sponsorship, and enhancing foundational literacy. Utilize change management principles to guide a phased approach—advancing at the pace of trust and alignment.

THE ASSESSMENT CAN BE DOWNLOADED AT:

www.cynthiabentzenmercer.com/resources

AFTERWORD

Afterword

THE BRIDGE BETWEEN
PERFORMANCE AND POSSIBILITY

This book has provided you with a framework: a practical, finance-minded approach to treating your people as the appreciating assets they are. However, before you close these pages, I want to leave you with something more profound, something that cannot be measured on a balance sheet but influences every number that appears there.

For over 30 years, I have sat in boardrooms and back offices, led multi-industry teams, and mentored individuals on the brink of burnout or the verge of breakthrough. Across every title, industry, and strategic plan, I have witnessed one undeniable truth: Organizations do not just employ people; they are entrusted with their potential.

Nevertheless, we manage human capital with far less discipline than we apply to financial capital. We make instinct-driven decisions about people while requiring data to justify a $10,000 budget shift. We debate the moral case for investing in people while quietly accepting the loss of talent we never truly recognized.

THE OPPORTUNITY COST
IS STAGGERING.

When we fail to recognize people as high-yield assets, we lose retention, innovation, trust, reputation, and growth. However, when we lead differently—when we invest wisely, strategically, and with intention—we unleash exponential value.

That is why I wrote this book..

This is not to reform HR or promote another leadership trend but to reframe human capital as the most overlooked driver of competitive advantage.

Because I believe that:

- Human capital and human dignity can coexist.
- Profitability and positive culture are not mutually exclusive.
- Every person has potential, and when aligned with purpose, they become unstoppable.

So, if this book has challenged how you lead, invest in, or account for the human capital entrusted to you, good. That means the work is just beginning.

LET THIS BE YOUR CALL TO ACTION.

Not just to manage. Not just to support.

BUT TO INVEST BOLDLY, WISELY, AND INTENTIONALLY.

Because that is how we build organizations worthy of the people who power them.

-Dr. Cynthia Bentzen-Mercer

GLOSSARY

Glossary OF TERMS

Ability: The capacity to perform the essential functions of a job.

Absenteeism Rate: Measures unplanned absences and their impact.

Accounting of Human Capital (AHC): An assessment of every individual's human capital (ability, ethos, knowledge, skills, natural talent), segmented by current performance and talent for the role.

ACES: An acronym used to describe the observational insights of an incumbent and assess an individual's natural talent for a role (affirmation, consistency, excellence, spontaneity).

Affinity Bias: A preference for those who look, act, or think like us.

Cost per Hire: The cost incurred in recruiting each new employee.

Depth Risk: Either planned attrition, such as retirement, promotion, or coaching out a poor performer, or unplanned attrition, including sudden departures or known flight risks, without a readily available and prepared successor.

Employee Engagement Score: The satisfaction of employees typically derived from surveys.

Employee Net Promoter Score (eNPS): Measures how likely employees are to recommend their workplace.

Ethos: The shared norms, guiding principles, values, and attitudes of an organization, actualized by who they select, develop, and promote.

Flight Risk: The risk of pros or high potentials exiting the organization based on poor leadership, limited growth, and lack of development opportunities.

Force Multiplier: An organization's ability to generate value beyond the sum of its individual contributors.

General Mental Ability (GMA): The mental skills related to spatial, numerical, mechanical, and verbal abilities.

Goal Achievement Rate: Percentage of key performance indicators (KPIs) employees meet.

Heterogeneity: The quality or state of consisting of dissimilar or diverse elements.

High Potential: A profile of an individual with strong talent for the position or role they are in, but not yet living up to their full capability.

Homogeneity: The quality or state of being of a similar kind or of having a uniform structure.

Human Capital: The unique abilities, skills, knowledge, talents, and experiences that every individual brings to bear.

Human Capital Portfolio (HCP): The collection of unique abilities, skills, knowledge, talents, and experiences that are represented in the composite of a group.

Human Capital ROI: Measures the return on investment in human capital, typically using formulas like (Revenue – Operating

Expenses) / Human Capital Costs.

Internal Mobility Rate: The frequency of employees moving to new roles within the company.

Knowledge: The information and understanding we acquire through education or experience.

Miscast: A profile of an individual who has soft performance and soft talent for the position or role they are currently in.

Neurodiversity: A framework for understanding human brain function that considers the diversity within sensory processing, motor abilities, social comfort, cognition, and focus as neurobiological differences.

New Hire Turnover Rate: The percentage of new hires leaving within a specific period (e.g., first 90 days).

Offer Acceptance Rate: The percentage of job offers accepted.

Path Forward: The action suggested to rebalance the Human Capital Portfolio based on each individual's persona in their current role (recast/exit, monitor, invest, optimize).

Performance Rating Distribution: The percentage of employees in different performance rating categories.

Predictive Validity: The ability of a test or other measurement to predict a future outcome.

Pro: A profile of an individual with strong talent and performance for their position or role.

Profit per Employee: The net profit divided by the number of employees.

Retention Rate: The percentage of employees retained over a specific period.

Revenue per Employee: The total revenue divided by the number of employees.

Regrettable Attrition: Avoidable, voluntary exit of pros and high potentials.

Requisite Ability: The mental and physical ability to perform the essential functions of the job.

Role Player: A profile of an individual who has soft natural talent for the position or role they are in but is able to meet the performance criteria.

Skills: The ability to demonstrate knowledge through application and practice.

Social Identity Theory: Explains how people categorize themselves and others into in-groups and out-groups.

Talent: That which the research community has generally named personality traits, i.e., stability of thoughts, feelings, and behaviors, as well as innate aptitude, i.e., that which comes naturally, without effort, and can be developed to near-perfect performance.

Time-to-Fill: The average time taken to fill open positions.

Voluntary vs. Involuntary Turnover: Breakdown of turnover by employee-initiated vs. employer-initiated departures.

Will: The motivation, desire, and personal commitment an individual brings to their role.

TOOLKIT

Toolkit

The collection of tools and templates are available to download free of charge at:

www.cynthiabentzenmercer.com/resources

 ## STEP 1
Establish Pro Forma:

- Human Capital Investment Strategy (HCIS) Framework
- HCIS Pro Forma

 ## STEP 2
Assess Portfolio

- Human Capital Investment Strategy (HCIS) Framework
- Human Capital Attributes Model
- ACES Talent Tool
- AHC Performance/Talent Matrix
- AHC Position Profile Matrix
- Predictive Validity of Assessments Graph

STEP 3
Stratify Risk

- Human Capital Investment Strategy (HCIS) Framework
- Depth Chart
- Flight Risk Chart
- Attrition Disruption Risk Evaluation
- Leader Risk Personas
- Risk Assessment

STEP 4
Rebalance Allocations

- Human Capital Investment Strategy (HCIS) Framework
- Accounting of Human Capital: Rebalancing Path Forward
- *Miscast* Position Profile
- *Role Player* Position Profile
- *High Potential* Position Profile
- *Pro* Position Profile

STEP 5
Expand Options

- Human Capital Investment Strategy (HCIS) Framework
- Accounting of Human Capital: Rebalancing Path Forward

STEP 6
Forecast & Adjust

- Human Capital Investment Strategy (HCIS) Framework
- Governance Outline

Enabling A HUMAN CAPITAL INVESTMENT CULTURE

- Human Capital Investment Strategy (HCIS) Framework
- Reaction to Change
- Change Management Strategy
- Leading Change Method
- Organizational Readiness Assessment

NOTES

Notes

AARP. (2018). The Value of Experience: Age Discrimination Against Older Workers Persists. https://employerportal.aarp.org/wp-content/uploads/2024/09/value-of-experience-age-discrimination-highlights_doi_10_26419-2Fres_00177_002.pdf

Achieving growth: Putting leadership mindsets and behaviors into action. McKinsey & Company. (2025, January 13). https://www.mckinsey.com/capabilities/growth-marketing-and-sales/our-insights/achieving-growth-putting-leadership-mindsets-and-behaviors-into-actionMcKinsey & Company+1McKinsey & Company+1

Adkins, A. (2015, April 13). Only One in 10 People Possess the Talent to Manage. Gallup. https://www.gallup.com/workplace/236579/one-people-possess-talent-manage.aspx

Barriere, M., Chase, L., & Sullivan, R. (2018, August 7). Winning with your talent-management strategy. McKinsey & Company. https://www.mckinsey.com/capabilities/people-and-organizational-performance/our-insights/winning-with-your-talent-management-strategy

Barriere, M., Chase, L., & Sullivan, R. (2018). Winning with your talent-management strategy [PDF]. McKinsey & Company. https://www.mckinsey.com/~/media/McKinsey/Business%20Functions/Organization/Our%20Insights/Winning%20with%20your%20talent%20management%20strategy/Winning-with-your-talent-management-strategy.pdfMcKinsey & Company+1McKinsey & Company+1

Barriere, M., Chase, L., & Sullivan, R. (2018). Linking talent to value.

McKinsey & Company. https://www.mckinsey.com/capabilities/
people-and-organizational-performance/our-insights/linking-talent-
to-valueMcKinsey & Company+1McKinsey & Company+1

Benson, A. M., Li, D., & Shue, K. (2024). "Potential" and the gender
promotion gap. Academy of Management Proceedings, 2023(1),
1–29. https://doi.org/10.5465/amproc.2023.19580abstract

Bentzen-Mercer, C. & Rath, K. K. (2024). Now, Near, Next: A Practical
Guide for Mid-Career Women to Move from Professional
Serendipity to Intentional Advancement.

Bersin, J. (2014, January 27). Becoming irresistible: A new model for
employee engagement. Deloitte Insights. https://www2.deloitte.
com/us/en/insights/deloitte-review/issue-16/employee-engagement-
strategies.html

Bidwell, M. (2011). Paying more to get less: The effects of external
hiring versus internal mobility. Administrative Science Quarterly,
56(3), 369–407. https://doi.org/10.1177/0001839211433562

Boushey, H., & Glynn, S. J. (2012, November 16). There are signif
icant business costs to replacing employees. Center for
American Progress. https://www.americanprogress.org/article/
there-are- significant-business-costs-to-replacing-employees/
Center for American Progress+1Center for American Prog
ress+1

Boston Consulting Group. (2024, January 23). Finding and keeping
the right talent for business building. https://www.bcg.com/
publications/2025/finding-and-keeping-the-right-talent-for-
growthBCG Global

Buckingham, M., & Clifton, D. O. (2001). Now, discover your strengths.
Free Press.

CareerBuilder. (2017, December 7). Nearly three in four employers affected by a bad hire, according to a recent CareerBuilder survey. PR Newswire. https://www.prnewswire.com/news-releases/nearly-three-in-four-employers-affected-by-a-bad-hire-according-to-a-recent-careerbuilder-survey-300567056.html

Choi-Allum, Lona. Age Discrimination Among Workers Age 50-Plus. Washington, DC: AARP Research, July 2022/January 2024. https://doi.org/10.26419/res.00545.001

Conaway, C. (2024, August 17). Textio's analysis of 23,000 performance feedback reviews exposed bias in the workplace. LinkedIn. https://www.linkedin.com/pulse/textios-analysis-23000-performance-feedback-reviews-exposed-conaway-w4s5c

Corporate Executive Board. (2016). Open source change: Making change management work. https://pwchangetoolkit.files.wordpress.com/2021/05/ceb_open_source_change_full_study-2-1.pdf

Correll, S. J., & Simard, C. (2016, April 29). Research: Vague feedback is holding women back. Harvard Business Review. https://hbr.org/2016/04/research-vague-feedback-is-holding-women-back

Culloo, J. (Oct. 31, 2023). Unlocking Success: The Importance of A-Players and the Cost of Retaining Underperformers | LinkedIn

Customer confidence. Gartner. (n.d.). https://www.gartner.com/en/sales/insights/customer-confidenceGartner

Dana, J., Dawes, R. M., & Peterson, N. (2013). Belief in the unstructured interview: The persistence of an illusion. Judgment and Decision Making, 8(5), 512–520. Cambridge University Press & Assessment+1ResearchGate+1

Deloitte. (2020). The social enterprise at work: Paradox as a path forward. Deloitte Insights. https://www2.deloitte.com/content/dam/Deloitte/tw/Documents/human-capital/tw-2020-human-capital-trends.pdf

Deloitte. (2023). 2023 Global Human Capital Trends: New fundamentals for a boundaryless world. Deloitte Insights. https://www2.deloitte.com/us/en/insights/focus/human-capital-trends/2023.html

Deloitte. (2024, May). 2Q24 CFO Signals Full Report. https://www2.deloitte.com/content/dam/Deloitte/us/Documents/us-2Q24-cfo-signals-full-report-final.pdf

Egon Zehnder. (2024, October). The CEO Response: Revealing Insights. https://www.egonzehnder.com/the-ceo-response

Future Forum. (2022, October). Executives feel the strain of leading in the 'new normal.' https://futureforum.com/research/pulse-report-fall-2022-executives-feel-strain-leading-in-new-normal/

Gallup. (n.d.). Employee engagement & experience. https://www.gallup.com/workplace/229424/employee-engagement.aspx

Gallup. (2019, May 20). Retain your top talent, don't hand them to competitors. https://www.gallup.com/cliftonstrengths/en/298787/retain-top-talent-don-hand-competitors.aspxGallup.com+1Gallup.com+1

Gallup. (2020, February 4). How to improve employee engagement in the workplace. https://www.gallup.com/workplace/285674/improve-employee-engagement-workplace.aspx

Gallup. (2024). State of the Global Workplace: 2024 Report. https://www.gallup.com/workplace/349484/state-of-the-global-workplace.aspx

Gallup & Workhuman. (2022). Recognition as a Business Imperative:

New Insights from Gallup and Workhuman. https://assets.
ctfassets.net/

Gartner. (2022, October 12). Gartner survey reveals leader and manager effectiveness tops HR leaders' list of priorities for 2023. https://www.gartner.com/en/newsroom/press-releases/2022-10-12-gartner-survey-reveals-leader-and-manager-effectiveness-tops-hr-leaders-list-of-priorities-for-2023

Green, J., & Hand, J. R. M. (2021, March 25). Measuring and calibrating the racial/ethnic densities of executives in US publicly traded companies [Working paper]. Kenan Institute of Private Enterprise. https://kenaninstitute.unc.edu/wp-content/uploads/2021/03/US-Exec-RAEDs-Green-Hand-20210325.pdf

Herzberg, F., Mausner, B., & Snyderman, B. B. (1959). The motivation to work (2nd ed.). New York: John Wiley & Sons.

Herzberg, F. (1968). One more time: How do you motivate employees? Harvard Business Review, 46(1), 53–62.

Hiatt, J. M. (2006). ADKAR: A model for change in business, government, and our community. Prosci Learning Center Publications.

Hunt, V., Prince, S., Dixon-Fyle, S., & Yee, L. (2020). Diversity wins: How inclusion matters. McKinsey & Company. https://www.mckinsey.com/featured-insights/diversity-and-inclusion/diversity-wins-how inclusion-mattersMcKinsey & Company+3McKinsey & Company+3McKinsey & Company+3

Hunter, J. E., Schmidt, F. L., & Judiesch, M. K. (1990). Individual differences in output variability as a function of job complexity. Journal of Applied Psychology, 75(1), 28–42. https://doi.org/10.1037/0021-9010.75.1.28

Jampol, L., Rattan, A., & Wolf, E. B. (2023, January 25). Women get "nicer" feedback — and it holds them back. Harvard Business Review. https://hbr.org/2023/01/women-get-nicer-feedback-and-it-holds-them-backHarvard Business Review

Kausel, E. E., Culbertson, S. S., & Madrid, H. P. (2016). Overconfidence in personnel selection: When and why unstructured interview information can hurt hiring decisions. Organizational Behavior and Human Decision Processes, 137, 27–44. https://doi.org/10.1016/j.obhdp.2016.07.005

Korn Ferry. (2018). Future of work: The global talent crunch. https://www.kornferry.com/insights/this-week-in-leadership/talent-crunch-future-of-workKorn Ferry+9

Kotter, J. P. (1995). Leading change: Why transformation efforts fail. Harvard Business Review, 73(2), 59–67. https://hbr.org/1995/05/leading-change-why-transformation-efforts-fail-2

Lean In & McKinsey & Company. (2022). Women in the Workplace 2022. https://www.mckinsey.com/featured-insights/diversity-and-inclusion/women-in-the-workplace

LinkedIn Talent Solutions. (2022, October). Hiring in 2023: How Talent Leaders Are Navigating a Changing Market. https://www.linkedin.com/business/talent/blog/talent-acquisition/hiring-2023-talent-leaders-navigate-changing-market

LinkedIn Learning. (2023). 2023 Workplace Learning Report: Building the Agile Future. https://learning.linkedin.com/resources/workplace-learning-report-2023

Lorenzo, R., Voigt, N., Schetelig, K., Zawadzki, A., Welpe, I., & Brosi, P. (2018). How diverse leadership teams boost innovation. Boston Consulting Group. https://www.bcg.com/publications/2018/how-diverse-leadership-teams-boost-innovationBCG Global

Lucas, S. (2024, December 17). Study: 88 percent of high-performing women get critiqued on their personalities in performance reviews. Inc. https://www.inc.com/suzanne-lucas/study-88-percent-of-high-performing-women-get-critiqued-on-their-personalities-in-performance-reviews/91065493Inc.com

Madgavkar, A., Schaninger, B., Maor, D., White, O., Smit, S., Samandari, H., Woetzel, J., Carlin, D., & Chockalingam, K. (2022, June). Human capital at work: The value of experience [PDF]. McKinsey Global Institute. https://www.mckinsey.com/~/media/mckinsey/business%20functions/people%20and%20organizational%20performance/our%20insights/human%20capital%20at%20work%20the%20value%20of%20experience/mgi-human-capital-report-jun2022.pdfMcKinsey & Company+3McKinsey & Company+3McKinsey & Company+3

Madgavkar, A., Schaninger, B., Maor, D., White, O., Smit, S., Samandari, H., Woetzel, J., Carlin, D., & Chockalingam, K. (2023, February 2). Performance through people: Transforming human capital into competitive advantage. McKinsey Global Institute. https://www.mckinsey.com/mgi/our-research/performance-through-people-transforming-human-capital-into-competitive-advantage

McKinsey & Company. (2018, August 7). Winning with your talent-management strategy. https://www.mckinsey.com/capabilities/people-and-organizational-performance/our-insights/winning-with-your-talent-management-strategy (McKinsey & Company & LeanIn Org, 2024)

McKinsey & Company. (2021, June 28). Making work meaningful from the C-suite to the frontline. https://www.mckinsey.com/capabilities/people-and-organizational-performance/our-insights/making-work-meaningful-from-the-c-suite-to-the-frontline

McKinsey & Company. (2021, September 8). The Great Attrition is making hiring harder. Are you searching the right talent pools? https://www.mckinsey.com/capabilities/people-and-organizational-performance/our-insights/the-great-attrition-is-making-hiring-harder-are-you-searching-the-right-talent-pools

McKinsey & Company. (2022, June 23). Americans are embracing flexible work—and they want more of it. https://www.mckinsey. com/industries/real-estate/our-insights/americans-are-embracing-flexible-work-and-they-want-more-of-it

McKinsey & Company. (2023, March 17). The critical role of strategic workforce planning in the age of AI. https://www.mckinsey. com/capabilities/people-and-organizational-performance/our-insights/the-critical-role-of-strategic-workforce-planning-in-the-age-of-ai

McKinsey & Company. (2023, April 26). The State of Organizations 2023: Ten shifts transforming organizations. https://www.mckinsey. com/capabilities/people-and-organizational-performance our-insights/the-state-of-organizations-2023

Mohr, T. S. (2014, August 25). Why women don't apply for jobs unless they're 100% qualified. Harvard Business Review. https:// hbr.org/2014/08/why-women-dont-apply-for-jobs-unless-theyre-100-qualified

Neumark, D., Burn, I., & Button, P. (2020). Older workers need not apply? Ageist language in job ads and age discrimination in hiring. National Bureau of Economic Research. https://www.nber.org/system/files/working_papers/w26552/w26552.pdf

Neumann, M., Niessen, A. S. M., & Meijer, R. R. (2021). Implementing evidence-based assessment and selection in organizations: A review and an agenda for future research. Organizational Psychology Review, 11(3), 205–239. https://doi. org/10.1177/2041386620983419

Nolan, Kevin P., Dalal, Dev K., and Carter, Nathan (2020). "Threat of Technological Unemployment, Use Intentions, and the Promotion of Structured Interviews in Personnel Selection," Personnel

Assessment and Decisions: Number 6: Iss. 2, Article 6. DOI: https://doi.org/10.25035/pad.2020.02.006

O'Boyle Jr., E. H., & Aguinis, H. (2012). "The Best and the Rest: Revisiting the Norm of Normality of Individual Performance." Personnel Psychology, 65(1), 79–119. https://doi.org/10.1111/j.1744-6570.2011.01239.x

Pew Research Center. (2024, December 10). Key labor force trends. https://www.pewresearch.org/social-trends/2024/12/10/key-labor-force-trends/

Pink, D. H. (2009). Drive: The surprising truth about what motivates us. Riverhead Books.

Prosci. (2024, March 1). 6 reasons why change management fails and how to avoid them. https://www.prosci.com/blog/why-change-management-fails

Rivera, L. A. (2015). Pedigree: How elite students get elite jobs. Princeton University Press.

Roth, Purvis, & Bobko (2010) A Meta-Analysis of Gender Group Differences for Measures of Job Performance in Field Studies, Volume 38, Issue 2. https://doi.org/10.1177/0149206310374774

S&P Global Market Intelligence. (2019). When women lead, firms win. https://www.spglobal.com/marketintelligence/en/news-insights/research/when-women-lead-firms-winS&P Global

Sackett, P. R., Zhang, C., Berry, C. M., & Lievens, F. (2022). Revisiting meta-analytic estimates of validity in personnel selection: Addressing systematic overcorrection for restriction of range. Journal of Applied Psychology, 107(11), 2040–2068. https://doi.org/10.1037/apl0000994Gwern+3PubMed+3C

Sackett, P. R., Zhang, C., Berry, C. M., & Lievens, F. (2022). Revisiting meta-analytic estimates of validity in personnel selection: Addressing systematic overcorrection for restriction of range. Journal of Applied Psychology, 107, 2040–2068. https://doi. org/10.1037/apl0000994

Sackett, P. R., Zhang, C., Berry, C. M., & Lievens, F. (2023). Revisit ing the design of selection systems in light of new findings regarding the validity of widely used predictors. Industrial and Organizational Psychology: Perspectives on Science and Prac tice, 16(3), 283–300.

Schmidt, F. L., & Hunter, J. E. (1998). The validity and utility of selection methods in personnel psychology: Practical and theoretical implications of 85 years of research findings. Psychological Bulletin, 124, 262–274. https://doi.org/10.1037/0033-2909.124.2.262

Society for Human Resource Management. (2012). Retaining talent: A guide to analyzing and managing employee turnover. https://www. shrm.org/content/dam/en/shrm/topics-tools/news/Retaining-Talent. pdf

Society for Human Resource Management. (2020, March 23). Reducing employee turnover with creative workplace solutions. https://www.shrm.org/topics-tools/news/all-things-work/reducing-employee-turnoverSHRM+1SHRM+1

Sucher, S. J., & Westner, M. M. (2022, December 8). What companies still get wrong about layoffs. Harvard Business Review. https://hbr. org/2022/12/what-companies-still-get-wrong-about-layoffs

The leadership gap: How to fix what your organization lacks. Center for Creative Leadership. (2025, March 1). https://www.ccl.org/ articles/leading-effectively-articles/leadership-gap-what-you-still-need/CCL+2CCL+2CCL+2

Tajfel, H., & Turner, J. C. (1979). An integrative theory of intergroup conflict. In W. G. Austin & S. Worchel (Eds.), The social psychology of intergroup relations (pp. 33–47). Monterey, CA: Brooks/Cole.

U.S. Bureau of Labor Statistics. (n.d.). Homepage. https://www.bls.gov

U.S. Census Bureau. (n.d.). U.S. Census Bureau. https://www.census.gov

U.S. Department of Justice. (n.d.). Americans with Disabilities Act of 1990, as amended. https://www.ada.gov/law-and-regs/ada/Ada.gov+1A

Wigert, B., & Agrawal, S. (2018, July 12). Employee burnout, part 1: The 5 main causes. Gallup. https://www.gallup.com/workplace/237059/employee-burnout-part-main-causes.aspx

Work Institute. (2023). 2023 Retention Report. https://info.workinstitute.com/hubfs/2023%20Retention%20Report/Work%20Institute%202023%20Retention%20Report.pdfinfo.workinstitute.com+3info.workinstitute.com+3info.workinstitute.com+3

World Economic Forum. (2024, January). The CEO: A Personal Reflection. https://www.weforum.org/publications/the-ceo-a-personal-reflection

ACKNOWLEDGMENTS

Acknowledgments

To:

My incredible children who support, encourage, and teach me daily,

My mentors, coaches, and sponsors, past and present, who have challenged and pushed me to keep growing,

The advanced readers who dedicated their time, talent, and wisdom to ensuring this book resonated with a broad audience: Keith Jones, Julie and Mark Lowe, Tanya Marion, Reggie Mebane, and Kimberly Rath,

Kristin Olson for embarking on a second book journey with me, this time as my dedicated editor and writing advisor,

Kendra Cagle for the beautiful layout and book design,

Heather E. McGowan for her guidance, encouragement, and support throughout my journey as an author, and

Naren Aryal, Lauren Magnussen, and the Amplify Publishing team for believing in my vision once again.

–Cynthia

SPECIAL CONTRIBUTORS

Special CONTRIBUTORS

Special thanks to the following individuals who generously shared their time, insight, and lived leadership experience. Their contributions enriched this book with real-world relevance and made the Human Capital Investment Strategy framework more actionable for leaders everywhere.

Gerard van Grinsven

Gerard van Grinsven, CEO/President of Lumera, is a distinguished executive known for his visionary leadership and cross-sector expertise in hospitality, healthcare, and real estate. His forward-thinking approach to operational excellence and emotionally engaged cultures has earned him recognition worldwide.

Van Grinsven earned two Malcolm Baldrige National Quality Awards—first with The Ritz-Carlton Hotel Company in 1999 and later with Henry Ford Health System in 2012. His career includes notable leadership roles at The Ritz-Carlton Hotel Company, the Mandarin Oriental Hotel in Bangkok, Henry Ford Health System, and as President and CEO of Cancer Treatment Centers of America.

In 2015, he founded The van Grinsven Hospitality Group, partnering with healthcare providers to pioneer a new model of hospitality grounded in wellness, safety, quality care, and human connection. In 2022, he became Chief Operating Officer at Waterstone Properties, championing a consumer-centric approach in healthcare design and experience.

Most recently, van Grinsven launched **Lumera**, a lifestyle brand redefining optimal living through the seamless integration of world-class hospitality and holistic well-being, setting a new global standard for purposeful, inspired living.

Shawn Layden

Shawn Layden's career with Sony Corporation lasted over three decades, the vast majority spent with PlayStation. He began his journey with Sony in 1987 in Tokyo, serving as a communications assistant to co-founder Akio Morita. Over the years, Layden held several key positions, including Vice President of Sony Computer Entertainment Europe, President of Sony Computer Entertainment Japan, and President and CEO of Sony Interactive Entertainment America (SIEA). In 2014, he became Chairman of SIEA Worldwide Studios, where he played a pivotal role in launching PlayStation consoles globally and led the establishment of PlayStation Productions to adapt game IPs into film and television. An alumnus of the University of Notre Dame, he continues to influence the gaming sector through advisory roles and mentorship, advocating for sustainable development practices and supporting initiatives like the Girls Make Games Scholarship Fund.

Reginald "Reggie" R. Mebane

Reggie Mebane is a transformational leader with over four decades of experience across the private and public sectors. His career spans 23 years at FedEx, rising from loading docks to Senior Vice President and COO of a $2B division, followed by 20 years in the federal government as a Senior Executive Service leader at the CDC. He has excelled in P&L management, organizational transformation, human capital strategy, and workforce engagement. Currently Vice Chair of Family Health Centers of Georgia and formerly a 13-year board member with Mercy Health System, Reggie brings deep governance expertise and strategic vision to his board service. He holds psychology degrees and Harvard Kennedy School executive certifications. A respected speaker on leadership and change management, his philosophy centers on creating impact and inspiring excellence with integrity.

ABOUT THE AUTHOR

About THE AUTHOR

Dr. Cynthia Bentzen-Mercer is a distinguished talent and organizational development strategist with over three decades of international executive leadership experience across multiple industries. She is the founder of Bentzen Performance Partners and co-founder of The Zeal of the Heel. Dr. Cynthia's expertise centers on her ability to actualize human potential, detailed in her *USA Today*–bestselling book, *Now, Near, Next: A Practical Guide for Mid-Career Women to Move from Professional Serendipity to Intentional Advancement*.

Dr. Cynthia holds a PhD in social psychology and an MBA. She is a Board Certified Coach (BCC) and a Senior Professional in Human Resources (SPHR). Her work with organizations such as Marriott, Hai Hospitality, Enhabit Home Health and Hospice, Athena Health, National Beer Wholesalers Association, Del Papa Distributing, the Sheehan Family Companies, and the Centers for Disease Control and Prevention (CDC) spans a range of services, including keynote presentations, C-suite executive coaching, and human capital consulting worldwide.

Her unique approach to maximizing human performance has been featured in *Improving HR* and Heather McGowan's *The Empathy Advantage*; on *The Seismic Shift* with Michelle Johnston; *This is Woman's Work* with Nicole Kalil; *The Chris Voss Show;* and in the *e-Missourian*, *The Business Journals*, *The Labor Tribune*, St. Louis Public Radio, and Catholic Health Association of the United States publications.

Her contributions have earned her recognition, including being featured in Ingram's "50 Missourians You Should Know," Becker's "143 Women Leaders of Hospital and Health Systems to Know," a St. Louis YWCA "Leader of Distinction," one of St. Louis's "Most Influential Businesswomen," and a 2024 recipient of "Women We Admire."

Blending her professional and philanthropic passions, Dr. Cynthia lends her time, talent, and treasure to organizations that focus on liberating those who are poor, underserved, or marginalized, including Dreams to Reality and AbleLight.

· ·